THE END TII
A Journey througn tne End of Days

Heather L. Rivard

Antichrist 2 Thess. 2v8
Daniel 9.v27   — ~~Heads~~
                      Heather p.56
Rev. 6v1

© 2016 Heather L. Rivard

All rights reserved. This book or parts thereof may not be reproduced in any form, stored in any retrieval system, or transmitted in any form by any means—electronic, mechanical, photocopy, recording, or otherwise—without prior written permission of the author, except as provided by United States of America copyright law.

Table of Contents

PART ONE: 6
The Battle of Gog and Magog 6

   Introduction 7
   What is the Point? 10
   What is the Battle of Gog and Magog? 14
      Ezekiel 38:1-23 (KJV) 16
   Who is Involved in the Battle of Gog and Magog? 23
   Why Will There be a Battle of Gog and Magog? 27
      How God's Purpose is Accomplished - Ezekiel 38 29
      Ezekiel 39:1-29 (KJV) 32
      How God's Purpose is Accomplished - Ezekiel 39 35
   What Will Israel's Role Be? 39
   Where Will the Battle of Gog and Magog Occur? 44
   When Will the Battle of Gog and Magog Occur? 49
   Final Thoughts 58

PART TWO: 59
The Daniel 9:27 Covenant 59

   An Overview of the 70 Weeks 60
   The Beginning of the 70th Week 63
      Who is "He"? 64
      What Does It Mean to "Confirm"? 72
      What is "the covenant"? 75
      Revelation's Sequence of Events 86
      Who Are the "Many"? 89
   The Middle of the 70th Week 92
      "He shall cause the sacrifice and the oblation to cease" 93

"And for the overspreading of abominations he shall make it desolate" 97
The End of the 70th Week 100
A Summary of Daniel 9:27 103
Final Thoughts 104

PART THREE: 106
The Feasts of the Lord 106

An Overview of the Feasts of the Lord 107
A Shadow of Things to Come 113
The Feast of Passover 115
The Feast of Unleavened Bread 117
The Feast of Firstfruits 120
The Feast of Weeks 122

   The Waiting Church 125

The Feast of Trumpets 128

   A Memorial of Blowing of Trumpets 129
   The Final Lawgiver 132

The Day of Atonement 135
The Feast of Tabernacles 142

   The Word Became Flesh 145

Final Thoughts 147

PART FOUR: 148
The Day of the Lord 148

The Purposes of the 70 Weeks of Daniel 149
At His Appearing and His Kingdom 154
The Light of the World 164

   The Glorious Appearing 167
   At evening time it shall be light 174

The 70 Weeks Completed 176

   To finish the transgression 178

    To make an end of sins 181
    To make reconciliation for iniquity 184
    To bring in everlasting righteousness 191
    The Prophesied Kingdom 198
    To seal up vision and prophecy 203
    To anoint the most holy 205
  Final Thoughts 215

PART FIVE: 216
The Final Jubilee Year 216
  An Overview of the End Times 217
  Restoration vs. Redemption 219
  The Prophecy in Ezekiel 40:1 224
    The Captivity and the Destruction of the City and Temple 225
  Entering the Promised Land 232
  The Reign of King Solomon 236
  The Exodus from Egypt 244
  The Jubilee Years from B.C. to A.D. 245
  The Final Jubilee Year – Revealed 246
  Final Thoughts 249
  Coming Soon!! 250
  About the Author 251
  References 252

PART ONE: The Battle of Gog and Magog

Introduction

As you may have guessed from the section title, there will be multiple parts to this book. My overall aim is to provide a comprehensive study of these last days and of the events which mark them. As I delve further into the subject matter you'll understand more clearly why I am beginning with the Battle of Gog and Magog.

I've tossed around the idea of writing a book for a while now, or at the very least doing some type of comprehensive study of the end times. I tried to start this a while back, but it kind of fell by the wayside. I had much more to learn before I came to the point I needed to be at to write this. In the interim, I've read some books, online articles, and blogs, as well as listened to a few different people speak on the different subjects involved in end times Bible prophecy. I've also delved into it quite a bit myself. I love to learn, and I love the process of learning. Those "a-ha moments" are wonderful, as they are proof our Lord is always with us and desires for us to seek and find Him.

> *Proverbs 25:2 (KJV) It is the glory of God to conceal a thing: but the honour of kings is to search out a matter.*[1]

I will never claim to know everything (and if anyone does claim to know everything, don't listen to them!). I won't even claim to know most things. I'm merely a student of the Word of God. I seek to know Him better through my study of His Word, and I seek to understand how soon we may get to meet our Jesus in the air.

The subject matter I most love to study is also some of the most highly debated. The content of this book expresses as much with the topics I've chosen to write about: The Battle of Gog and Magog; the Daniel 9:27 Covenant; The Feasts of the Lord; the Day of the Lord; and, the Final Jubilee year. These topics form an "end times timeline" of sorts, which is why this book was thusly named.

As we venture along together, please bear in mind I am coming at this from a pre-tribulational and premillennial viewpoint. Even if you don't agree with me, it will help if you understand my views prior to reading this so we can at least be on the same page for the moment. I am also a dispensationalist and fully believe God has different manners in which He deals with specific people groups in specific periods of time to achieve specific outcomes. If we don't understand that or try to confuse things, we will leave many things open to different interpretations that, quite frankly, neither need to be nor should be left open for interpretation. For those of you who may be unfamiliar with dispensationalism, I'll discuss points of it in greater detail as I go through this study.

The Bible is a very specific and very matter-of-fact point of reference. Our Lord's plans for His people, both Israel and the church, are very direct, very definitive, and very set-in-stone. His plans are all there for us to learn about, and it is best if we attempt to interpret things as He intended for us to rather than in a way that allows us to stick with any preconceived notions we might have. This is the difference between exegesis and eisegesis. Proper exegesis is what I have striven for.

Bible prophecy is a broad field. In Part One of this study, I will start with what has come to be called "The Battle of Gog and Magog". This battle seems to be front and center in many people's minds and vocabulary. There are many different viewpoints about this battle, especially regarding its timing. Some believe it will take place before the final seven years of history, also referred to as Daniel's 70th Week. Some believe The Battle of Gog and Magog will occur sometime shortly after the start of Daniel's 70th Week. Some believe it will occur in the middle of the 70th Week. Some believe it will occur at the end of Daniel's 70th Week. Some believe it will occur after Jesus's Millennial Reign on earth. By the end of this study, you will not only understand why I believe what I believe about the timing of this battle, but you will also understand why some of these lines of thought will wind up disqualifying themselves. I'll explain more about that as I go.

For now, to understand why different schools of thought exist and why they differ so greatly, we will need to approach the subject in five different ways – what, who, why, where, and when. I think after I proceed through these "five w's", we'll have a much better understanding of how it is likely this conflict will play out. Essentially, understanding the game plan comes down to understanding why things need to play out the way they do. This isn't about how things "could" play out, but rather understanding why events need to occur in a certain manner. The achievement of such understanding is my entire premise for writing this.

I'm getting a bit ahead of myself. Before I explain why things need to play out in a certain manner, I need to walk you through the "what" portion of the Battle of Gog and Magog. Please allow me to start laying the foundation for my entire End Times Timeline by helping you understand why you should care.

What is the Point?

Why should we care about "The Battle of Gog and Magog"? I cannot speak for the secular community, because I am not a member of it. However, I would be hard-pressed to think anyone who reads the news with any regularity hasn't been made at least a little aware of what is going on in the Middle East. Whether the secular community chooses to care is beyond the scope of this study. At the end of the day, we should all know God's prophetic clock stops for no one. Thus, as part of the body of Christ, we should desire to know where we are with respect to the end of days.

Found in the pages of Ezekiel, we read about a battle that was prophesied to occur in the "latter days". It should be noted Ezekiel was alive during the fall of Jerusalem that led to Israel's Babylonian Captivity around 607 B.C. For purposes of this part of the paper, 607 B.C. isn't especially important. However, it will become very important in Part Five when I discuss the final jubilee year.

You may be familiar with the Biblical prophet Daniel, of whom Ezekiel was a contemporary. The book of Daniel contains the famous prophetic chapter and verses from whence we derive the phrase "The 70 Weeks of Daniel".

> *Daniel 9:24 Seventy weeks are determined upon thy people and upon thy holy city, to finish the transgression, and to make an end of sins, and to make reconciliation for iniquity, and to bring in everlasting righteousness, and to seal up the vision and prophecy, and to anoint the most Holy. 25 Know therefore and understand, that from the going forth of the commandment to restore and to build Jerusalem unto the Messiah the Prince shall be seven weeks, and threescore and two weeks: the street shall be built again, and the wall, even in troublous times. 26 And after threescore and two weeks*

shall Messiah be cut off, but not for himself: and the people of the prince that shall come shall destroy the city and the sanctuary; and the end thereof shall be with a flood, and unto the end of the war desolations are determined. 27 And he shall confirm the covenant with many for one week: and in the midst of the week he shall cause the sacrifice and the oblation to cease, and for the overspreading of abominations he shall make it desolate, even until the consummation, and that determined shall be poured upon the desolate.[2]

The first 69 Weeks of years have already been fulfilled. The decree to restore and rebuild Jerusalem was given by Artaxerxes on March 14, 445 B.C. From there, a day count of 173,880 days ends us up at Palm Sunday, April 6, 32 A.D.[3]

7 Weeks x 7 years per Week x 360 days per year = 17,640 days
62 Weeks x 7 years per Week x 360 days per year = 156,240 days

17,640 + 156,240 = 173,880 days in 69 Weeks

It was at the end of that very day count, on Palm Sunday, Jesus rode into Jerusalem on a donkey, and presented Himself as the Lamb of God who would be sacrificed on Passover, four days later.

Matthew 21:5 Tell ye the daughter of Sion, Behold, thy King cometh unto thee, meek, and sitting upon an ass, and a colt the foal of an ass. 6 And the disciples went, and did as Jesus commanded them, 7 And brought the ass, and the colt, and put on them their clothes, and they set him thereon. 8 And a very great multitude spread their garments in the way; others cut down branches from the trees, and strawed them in the way. 9 And the multitudes that went before, and that followed, cried, saying, Hosanna to the son of David: Blessed is he that cometh in the name of the Lord; Hosanna in the highest. 10 And when he was come into Jerusalem, all the city was moved, saying, Who is this? 11 And the multitude said, This is Jesus the prophet of Nazareth of Galilee.[4]

Daniel 9:26 tells us after the conclusion of the first 69 Weeks, Messiah would be "cut off", or killed, but not for Himself. Rather, He laid down His life for us, taking upon Himself the sins of the world. Thus, the New Covenant was established, and the "age of grace", also referred to as the church age, was born. In the stopping of the progression of those Weeks of years, we realize quickly one final Week of years remains unfulfilled. The final Week is the focus of Daniel 9:27.

Daniel 9:27 And he shall confirm the covenant with many for one week: and in the midst of the week he shall cause the sacrifice and the oblation to cease, and for the overspreading of abominations he shall make it desolate, even until the consummation, and that determined shall be poured upon the desolate.

In the context of the end of days, and specifically regarding Ezekiel 38-39, it is the last verse of Daniel 9 which is in view. Verse 27 details the events of this final, yet unfilled Week of the "70 Weeks" prophecy.

Why is Daniel 9:27 important?

Because it tells us about several key events which will immediately precede the Second Coming of Jesus Christ. Yet, even as these events will all precede the Second Coming of Jesus Christ, not one of them will precede the rapture of the church. Furthermore, because the rapture of the church is a "sign-less" event, we must then use our knowledge of the timing of the events which will occur during the 70th Week to approximate how much closer we then must be to the rapture. This is a benefit of dispensational theology. If we see those events being lined up now, how much closer must we then be to our "blessed hope"? It is our "blessed hope" which will set the rest of the events into motion.

> *Titus 2:13 Looking for that blessed hope, and the glorious appearing of the great God and our Saviour Jesus Christ; 14 Who gave himself for us, that he might redeem us from all iniquity, and purify unto himself a peculiar people, zealous of good works.[5]*

That's great! But how do we have any idea where we are on God's prophetic time clock to even begin suggesting the rapture of the church is remotely close? This is where the prophecy found in Ezekiel 38-39 enters in.

The purpose of starting this timeline with the Battle of Gog and Magog is to help us understand when, if only approximately, this conflict will occur, why it needs to happen, when it needs to happen, who is involved, where it will occur, and what will result from it, not necessarily in that order. When we understand its place in Biblical eschatology, we can further approximate the lateness of the prophetic hour. We will begin by looking at the "what" aspect of this end times conflict.

What is the Battle of Gog and Magog?

Before I get to the prophecies detailed in Ezekiel 38-39, it is pertinent to point out the sequential nature of the chapters in Ezekiel. From this, we can understand Israel will have first been gathered back into her land prior to the conflict detailed in chapters 38-39. We learn as much from the events detailed in Ezekiel 36-37. We also learn of this in the Olivet Discourse given by Jesus in Matthew 24.

> *Matthew 24:32 Now learn a parable of the fig tree; When his branch is yet tender, and putteth forth leaves, ye know that summer is nigh: 33 So likewise ye, when ye shall see all these things, know that it is near, even at the doors. 34 Verily I say unto you, This generation shall not pass, till all these things be fulfilled.*[6]

Ezekiel 36 gives us more detail regarding the "fig tree", which is a symbol of national Israel.

> *Ezekiel 36:8 But ye, O mountains of Israel, ye shall shoot forth your branches, and yield your fruit to my people of Israel; for they are at hand to come. 9 For, behold, I am for you, and I will turn unto you, and ye shall be tilled and sown: 10 And I will multiply men upon you, all the house of Israel, even all of it: and the cities shall be inhabited, and the wastes shall be builded: 11 And I will multiply upon you man and beast; and they shall increase and bring fruit: and I will settle you after your old estates, and will do better unto you than at your beginnings: and ye shall know that I am the Lord. 12 Yea, I will cause men to walk upon you, even my people Israel; and they shall possess thee, and thou shalt be their inheritance, and thou shalt no more henceforth bereave them of men.*[7]

We learn of the same in Ezekiel 37, with the "dry bones" prophecy.

> *Ezekiel 37:11 Then he said unto me, Son of man, these bones are the whole house of Israel: behold, they say, Our bones are dried, and our hope is lost: we are cut off for our parts. 12 Therefore prophesy and say unto them, Thus saith the Lord God; Behold, O my people, I will open your graves, and cause you to come up out of your graves, and bring you into the land of Israel. 13 And ye shall know that I am the Lord, when I have opened your graves, O my people, and brought you up out of your graves, 14 And shall put my spirit in you, and ye shall live, and I shall place you in your own land: then shall ye know that I the Lord have spoken it, and performed it, saith the Lord.*[8]

Per the sequence of chapters in Ezekiel, after Israel has been gathered back into her land, a period of times will elapse, leading to the events detailed in Ezekiel 38-39. Ezekiel 40-48 then detail events which will occur at and after the Second Coming of Jesus Christ. We will discuss Ezekiel 40 in greater detail in Part Five of this End Times Timeline. However, from this sequence of chapters and their corresponding events, we can understand Ezekiel 38-39 is a latter-day prophecy. In fact, the prophecy tells us as much. Let's look at the first of the two chapters.

Ezekiel 38:1-23 (KJV)[9]

*1 And the word of the L*ORD *came unto me, saying, 2 Son of man, set thy face against Gog, the land of Magog, the chief prince of Meshech and Tubal, and prophesy against him, 3 And say, Thus saith the Lord G*OD*; Behold, I am against thee, O Gog, the chief prince of Meshech and Tubal: 4 And I will turn thee back, and put hooks into thy jaws, and I will bring thee forth, and all thine army, horses and horsemen, all of them clothed with all sorts of armour, even a great company with bucklers and shields, all of them handling swords: 5 Persia, Ethiopia, and Libya with them; all of them with shield and helmet: 6 Gomer, and all his bands; the house of Togarmah of the north quarters, and all his bands: and many people with thee. 7 Be thou prepared, and prepare for thyself, thou, and all thy company that are assembled unto thee, and be thou a guard unto them. 8 After many days thou shalt be visited: in the latter years thou shalt come into the land that is brought back from the sword, and is gathered out of many people, against the mountains of Israel, which have been always waste: but it is brought forth out of the nations, and they shall dwell safely all of them. 9 Thou shalt ascend and come like a storm, thou shalt be like a cloud to cover the land, thou, and all thy bands, and many people with thee. 10 Thus saith the Lord G*OD*; It shall also come to pass, that at the same time shall things come into thy mind, and thou shalt think an evil thought: 11 And thou shalt say, I will go up to the land of unwalled villages; I will go to them that are at rest, that dwell safely, all of them dwelling without walls, and having neither bars nor gates, 12 To take a spoil, and to take a prey; to turn thine hand upon the desolate places that are now inhabited, and upon the people that are gathered out of the nations, which have gotten cattle and goods, that dwell in the midst of the land. 13 Sheba, and Dedan, and the merchants of Tarshish, with all the young lions thereof, shall* *say unto thee, Art thou come to take a spoil? hast thou gathered thy company to take a prey? to carry away silver and gold, to take away cattle and goods, to take a great spoil? 14 Therefore, son of man, prophesy and say unto Gog, Thus saith the Lord G*OD*; In that day when my people of Israel dwelleth safely, shalt thou not know it? 15 And thou shalt come from thy place out of the north parts, thou, and many people with thee, all of them riding upon horses, a great company, and a mighty army: 16 And thou shalt come up against my people of Israel, as a cloud to cover the land; it shall be in the latter days, and I will bring thee against my land, that the heathen may know me, when I shall be sanctified in thee, O Gog, before their eyes. 17 Thus saith the Lord G*OD*; Art thou he of whom I have spoken in old time by my servants the prophets of Israel, which prophesied in those days many years that I would bring thee against them? 18 And it shall come to pass at the same time when Gog shall come against the land of Israel, saith the Lord G*OD*, that my fury shall come up in my face. 19 For in my jealousy and in the fire of my wrath have I spoken, Surely in that day there shall be a great shaking in the land of Israel; 20 So that the fishes of the sea, and the fowls of the heaven, and the beasts of the field, and all creeping things that creep upon the earth, and all the men that are upon the face of the earth, shall shake at my presence, and the mountains shall be thrown down, and the steep places shall fall, and every wall shall fall to the ground. 21 And I will call for a sword against him throughout all my mountains, saith the Lord G*OD*: every man's sword shall be against his brother. 22 And I will plead against him with pestilence and with blood; and I will rain upon him, and upon his bands, and upon the many people that are with him, an overflowing rain, and great hailstones, fire, and brimstone. 23 Thus will I magnify myself, and sanctify myself; and I will be known in the eyes of many nations, and they shall know that I am the L*ORD*.*

Since this portion of the study will detail the "what" aspect, let's look at what this prophecy entails. The aim of the conflict can be found in verses 7-12.

> *7 Be thou prepared, and prepare for thyself, thou, and all thy company that are assembled unto thee, and be thou a guard unto them. 8 After many days thou shalt be visited: in the latter years thou shalt come into the land that is brought back from the sword, and is gathered out of many people, against the mountains of Israel, which have been always waste: but it is brought forth out of the nations, and they shall dwell safely all of them. 9 Thou shalt ascend and come like a storm, thou shalt be like a cloud to cover the land, thou, and all thy bands, and many people with thee. 10 Thus saith the Lord God; It shall also come to pass, that at the same time shall things come into thy mind, and thou shalt think an evil thought: 11 And thou shalt say, I will go up to the land of unwalled villages; I will go to them that are at rest, that dwell safely, all of them dwelling without walls, and having neither bars nor gates, 12 To take a spoil, and to take a prey; to turn thine hand upon the desolate places that are now inhabited, and upon the people that are gathered out of the nations, which have gotten cattle and goods, that dwell in the midst of the land.*

In the latter days, there will be a massive army which will come against Israel with the aim of robbing her. We will get to the "who" in just a bit, but the reference is clear this army will seek to "take a spoil" and to "take a prey" from Israel. Israel will have, by the time this army arises, increased herself with some sort of wealth the invading army seeks to deprive her of. It should be made perfectly clear the goal of this end times invasion is not to wipe Israel off the map or to take her out of remembrance, as compared to the often-referenced Psalm 83. Rather, the goal of the Ezekiel 38-39 coalition is to steal something from her.

There is conjecture about what "the spoil" will be that this invading army seeks to take. Most believe it will be the oil and natural gas which Israel has recently found in great abundance. I would conjecture "the spoil" is not actually material wealth, but rather the very thing which seems to be at the heart of the spiritual battle constantly being waged. Perhaps the oil and natural gas will be ancillary, but I believe the true nature of the battle regards the very city which bears the name of God. It is the city which Jesus will rule and reign from when He establishes His Kingdom on earth. The city is none other than Jerusalem.

This idea may be new to many, but here is an excerpt taken from www.promisedlandministries.wordpress.com which may help to better understand the nature of this "spoil" which the Ezekiel 38-39 armies will seek to take from Israel.

> *Do you remember when you were a child, and somebody would take something from you? Sometimes, you would say, "Hey, that's not yours!" Then the reply would come: "It doesn't have your name on it!" This is often a battle between siblings when both want the same thing, but there isn't enough to go around. At least I've heard that a few times in my household.*
>
> *In Deuteronomy, when the Israelites were nearing the time of coming into the Promised Land, Moses was instructing them. Many instructions had been given by God in previous books, and Deuteronomy is basically Moses 'going back over' these things before the people journeyed forth into the land God gave them.*

In the 12th chapter of Deuteronomy, there are several references to the place that God would require them to meet with Him, bringing their sacrifices and offerings:

Deut 12:11 Then to the place the Lord your God will choose as a dwelling for his Name—there you are to bring everything I command you: your burnt offerings and sacrifices, your tithes and special gifts, and all the choice possessions you have vowed to the Lord.

Deut 12:21 If the place where the Lord your God chooses to put his Name is too far away from you, you may slaughter animals from the herds and flocks the Lord has given you, as I commanded you, and in your own towns you may eat as much of them as you want.

Jerusalem was the place to come and offer their gifts and sacrifices. This is where the tabernacle was, (and the temple came to be later) where sacrifices and offerings were made daily. There is great significance to this place. God was known by Abraham, Isaac, and Jacob as El Shaddai. Shaddai means 'almighty'. To them, God was called the 'Almighty God'.

The first letter of 'Shaddai' in Hebrew is the letter shin (pronounced 'sheen'). It looks like this:

The photo shows what shin looks like in book type. Just as in English, some of the Hebrew letters look different handwritten than they do in book type. To see a good representation of the letter shin in handwritten form, hold up

3 fingers just like you're trying to show someone the number 3. This gives a better picture of how it would have been written.[10]

Below is a picture to help illustrate the points being made above.

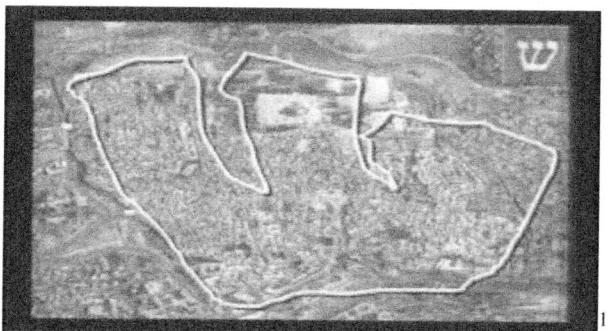
[11]

There is also conjecture the intended land area which this invading army will attempt to plunder is not actually Israel. I would beg to differ, especially considering the prophecies in chapters 36-37 specifically regard the desolate mountains of Israel and how they will be caused, by the hand of God, to be made fruitful. This fruitfulness will apply to both the people gathering back to the land and to the sustenance the land will produce for those people. Further, Israel is the only nation which has a covenant with God. We will see later God intervenes and makes a great showing of Himself on her behalf.

To further delve into the "what" aspect, we know from verse 4 that God, Himself, will determine the timing of this conflict. We are told God will place a "hook in the jaw" and lead these armies against Israel at His appointed time.

4 And I will turn thee back, and put hooks into thy jaws, and I will bring thee forth, and all thine army, horses and

> *horsemen, all of them clothed with all sorts of armour, even a great company with bucklers and shields, all of them handling swords:*

We must understand He is not forcing the battle to occur against the participants' wills. Rather, God is forcing it to occur at a time which He has predetermined. We know this from verse 17.

> *17 Thus saith the Lord God; Art thou he of whom I have spoken in old time by my servants the prophets of Israel, which prophesied in those days many years that I would bring thee against them?*

We also know this from Ezekiel 39:8:

> *8 Behold, it is come, and it is done, saith the Lord GOD; this is the day whereof I have spoken.*[12]

As we go through the text of these chapters, it will become abundantly clear "why" God is forcing the armies to come against Israel at an appointed time. We will continue discussing the "what" aspect a bit more as we talk about "who" is involved.

Who is Involved in the Battle of Gog and Magog?

The very first verses of Chapter 38 tell us who the parties involved will be. While there are a multitude of opinions regarding exactly who is intended, we are given insight into the main players.

> *1 And the word of the Lord came unto me, saying, 2 Son of man, set thy face against Gog, the land of Magog, the chief prince of Meshech and Tubal, and prophesy against him, 3 And say, Thus saith the Lord God; Behold, I am against thee, O Gog, the chief prince of Meshech and Tubal:*

There is a bit of debate about Gog being referred to as a "chief prince". If one reads the Septuagint, Gog is not actually referred to as the "chief prince of Meshech and Tubal". Rather, he is referred to as the "ruler of Rosh, Meshech, and Tubal". There is a significant difference regarding the placement of the word "chief". In Hebrew, "chief" is the word "rosh", and it is a noun. In the context of the King James, "rosh" is being used to describe Gog as a "chief" prince, seemingly indicating there is more than one "prince", with Gog being the chief of them. Rather, the intent here is to describe Gog as a prince of a specific geographical area: Rosh, Meshech, and Tubal.

    We see from other passages, specifically in Daniel, supernatural entities rule over specific geographical locations. For example, Daniel 10:20 refers both to the "prince of Grecia" and the "prince of Persia". Daniel 12:1 refers to Michael as the "great prince that standeth for the children of thy people", or Israel. Ephesians 2:2 refers to Satan as the "prince of the power of the air". In Daniel 9:26, the Antichrist is referred to as the "prince" of the people who would come and destroy the city and the sanctuary. Finally, Jesus is referred to, also in Daniel 9:26, as "Messiah the Prince". I use those examples to illustrate the accuracy of placement regarding the word "rosh". Gog, the leader of this latter-day army, is not the "chief/rosh" prince. Rather, he is the "prince of Rosh", Meshech, and Tubal.

It is incumbent upon me to differentiate this incursion of Gog from the second one we read about in Revelation 20. Revelation 20 gives an account of a second invasion of Gog after the Millennial Reign of Christ. The second invasion will be the final separation of believers and unbelievers who will either go into eternity with Jesus or be cast into the lake of fire at the Great White Throne judgment. Thus, Ezekiel's account is separated from Revelation 20's account by at least 1007 years. You may recall my earlier statement about the sequence of chapters in Ezekiel and how Ezekiel 40 <u>begins</u> the Millennial Reign of Christ on earth. Therefore, the Revelation 20 account, which takes place <u>after</u> the Millennial Reign, cannot be the same. However, we do learn a key detail about Gog from the second mention of him in Revelation: Gog is a supernatural entity. This further supports the idea of Gog being the "prince" of a geographical area, just as the other supernatural "princes" are.

> *5 Persia, Ethiopia, and Libya with them; all of them with shield and helmet: 6 Gomer, and all his bands; the house of Togarmah of the north quarters, and all his bands: and many people with thee.*

Persia is modern-day Iran. It is probably the least difficult of the names listed in verse 5 to guess. Ethiopia and Libya are linked to the ancient land areas of Cush and Phut. In modernity, they are most often linked to the North African nations of Libya and Sudan, perhaps also including Ethiopia. Gomer and Togarmah are typically linked to Turkey. Magog, which is mentioned in verse 2, is generally believed to be associated with the Muslim "-stan" nations. Considering the last clause of verse 6 says *"and many people with thee"*, it is likely people will continue to guess exactly who will be involved right up to the point we know for sure, which is to say, when the conflict occurs.

Below is a map of the land areas potentially represented by the players listed in Ezekiel 38-39.

I will point out, while I don't agree with the whole of this map regarding all the possible land areas identified, it does give what I believe to be a largely accurate display of all the land areas mentioned and where the armies will come from. Also of note regarding the players mentioned, aside from Iran, are their ancient progenitors. We find them mentioned in Genesis 10.

> *Genesis 10:2 The sons of Japheth; Gomer, and Magog, and Madai, and Javan, and Tubal, and Meshech, and Tiras. 3 And the sons of Gomer; Ashkenaz, and Riphath, and Togarmah.*[14]

Japheth was the father of Gomer, Magog, Tubal, Meshech, and as well as the grandfather of Togarmah.

> *Genesis 10:6 And the sons of Ham; Cush, and Mizraim, and Phut, and Canaan. 7 And the sons of Cush; Seba, and*

> *Havilah, and Sabtah, and Raamah, and Sabtechah: and the sons of Raamah; Sheba, and Dedan.*[15]

Ham was the father of Cush and Phut, as well as the great-grandfather of Sheba and Dedan. Although I have not yet mentioned Sheba and Dedan, I will refer to them momentarily.

It would seem as though this conflict is a play on the ancient brother vs. brother battle, originating with Cain vs. Abel, and further playing out with Ishmael vs. Isaac and Esau vs. Jacob. Israel is of the line of Shem, and those who will seek to come against her are cousins from the lines of Ham and Japheth.

The next people groups listed, in verse 13, are those which include Sheba and Dedan.

> *13 Sheba, and Dedan, and the merchants of Tarshish, with all the young lions thereof, shall say unto thee, Art thou come to take a spoil? hast thou gathered thy company to take a prey? to carry away silver and gold, to take away cattle and goods, to take a great spoil?*

What role do Sheba and Dedan play? The role of protestors. That's it. These people groups don't help Israel or harm her; they just seemingly complain about what is about to be done by Gog's army. Sheba and Dedan are modern-day Yemen and Saudi Arabia. The "merchants of Tarshish" is likely a reference to Britain, with the "young lions thereof" possibly being a reference to the United States and Australia. Regardless, all they do is recognize a conflict is coming and question or complain about the motivations of those coming against Israel. They do not offer support.

Then the invasion begins.

Why Will There be a Battle of Gog and Magog?

The next verses in Ezekiel 38 will begin to identify the purpose for this conflict. We will revisit this in greater detail when we get to Ezekiel 39.

> *14 Therefore, son of man, prophesy and say unto Gog, Thus saith the Lord God; In that day when my people of Israel dwelleth safely, shalt thou not know it? 15 And thou shalt come from thy place out of the north parts, thou, and many people with thee, all of them riding upon horses, a great company, and a mighty army: 16 And thou shalt come up against my people of Israel, as a cloud to cover the land; it shall be in the latter days, and I will bring thee against my land, that the heathen may know me, when I shall be sanctified in thee, O Gog, before their eyes. 17 Thus saith the Lord God; Art thou he of whom I have spoken in old time by my servants the prophets of Israel, which prophesied in those days many years that I would bring thee against them?*

I mentioned God has ordained this conflict to occur at a specific time. Verse 14 tells us as much when using the phrase *"that day"*. Ezekiel 38:17 refers to *"those days many years"*, or to the latter days. Furthermore, Ezekiel 39:8b says *"this is the day whereof I have spoken"*.

At this prophesied time, and via the "hook in the jaw" God places to draw Gog and Gog's army down to Israel, it appears the world will wait on baited breath to see what is about to occur. Gog and Gog's army will come against Israel, a people who have been gathered back into the land and dwell there securely. Gog will attempt to invade and plunder her with an army so massive it is described as "a cloud to cover the land".

Just as Gog has a purpose for coming against Israel, God has a purpose for allowing it. Actually, God has two purposes. The first is initially referenced in Ezekiel 38:16 - *"that the heathen may know me"*. The other purpose regards Israel. Within the context of both chapters, this purpose is specified five times. The other four are as follows:

> *Ezekiel 38:23 Thus will I magnify myself, and sanctify myself; and I will be known in the eyes of many nations, and they shall know that I am the Lord.*
>
> *Ezekiel 39:7 So will I make my holy name known in the midst of my people Israel; and I will not let them pollute my holy name any more: and the heathen shall know that I am the Lord, the Holy One in Israel.*[16]
>
> *Ezekiel 39:13b and it shall be to them a renown the day that I shall be glorified, saith the Lord God.*[17]
>
> *Ezekiel 39:21 And I will set my glory among the heathen, and all the heathen shall see my judgment that I have executed, and my hand that I have laid upon them.*[18]

This conflict is allowed in order that God, through His actions on behalf of Israel, can do two things:

1. Be known among the heathen
2. Elicit a specific response from Israel

We will discuss the second purpose in greater detail when we get to the end of Ezekiel 39.

How God's Purpose is Accomplished - Ezekiel 38

The next verses of Ezekiel 38 describe the "how" of this conflict. After the armies seeking to come against Israel begin to do so, God will stop them dead in their tracks. I mean that very literally.

> *18 And it shall come to pass at the same time when Gog shall come against the land of Israel, saith the Lord God, that my fury shall come up in my face. 19 For in my jealousy and in the fire of my wrath have I spoken, Surely in that day there shall be a great shaking in the land of Israel; 20 So that the fishes of the sea, and the fowls of the heaven, and the beasts of the field, and all creeping things that creep upon the earth, and all the men that are upon the face of the earth, shall shake at my presence, and the mountains shall be thrown down, and the steep places shall fall, and every wall shall fall to the ground. 21 And I will call for a sword against him throughout all my mountains, saith the Lord God: every man's sword shall be against his brother. 22 And I will plead against him with pestilence and with blood; and I will rain upon him, and upon his bands, and upon the many people that are with him, an overflowing rain, and great hailstones, fire, and brimstone.*

I think it's fair to say God will not appreciate what is on the hearts and minds of the army coming against His people. Therefore, He will act without mercy against them. I will also explore these verses in a bit of a different context when I discuss the timing of this conflict, because I believe there is a significant dispensational aspect to them. Keep that thought in your back pocket for now, because I will offer much greater detail to support this conclusion. However, it isn't for just yet.

In verse 18, we have the presence of God's fury, and in verse 19, the presence of His wrath. The Hebrew word for "fury" is "chemah"[19]. The Hebrew word for "wrath" is "ebrah"[20]. When doing a study of the Hebrew to the Greek, we can find an example of usage of the word "thymós"[21], which is "fury" in Greek, and the word "orgḗ"[22], which is "wrath" in Greek, in the following verse:

> *Revelation 16:19 And the great city was divided into three parts, and the cities of the nations fell: and great Babylon came in remembrance before God, to give unto her the cup of the wine of the fierceness (thymós) of his wrath (orgḗ).*[23]

Thus, we can say His wrath is caused by His fury, or it is His "furious wrath". Regardless, He acts on that feeling. As a dispensationalist, I am quite certain God would not act in such a capacity if the church were still here at that point. After all, I Thessalonians 5:5, 9-10 tell us as much.

> *I Thessalonians 5:5 Ye are all the children of light, and the children of the day: we are not of the night, nor of darkness. 9 For God hath not appointed us to wrath, but to obtain salvation by our Lord Jesus Christ, 10 Who died for us, that, whether we wake or sleep, we should live together with him.*[24]

At His appointed time, the army which seeks to take from Israel what is not theirs to take will experience the wrath of God. First, an earthquake will occur in the land of Israel. Said earthquake will be so massive, all the following will be made to shake at the presence of God:

- The fishes of the sea
- The fowls of the air
- The beasts of the field
- The creeping things
- The men that are upon the earth
- The mountains

- The ravines
- All the walls

Fear and confusion will strike the members of this army, and they will turn their swords upon one another. Those who do not kill each other will have their lives ended by God in one of six different ways:

> *22 And I will plead against him with pestilence and with blood; and I will rain upon him, and upon his bands, and upon the many people that are with him, an overflowing rain, and great hailstones, fire, and brimstone.*

The entire army will be destroyed.

> *Ezekiel 38:23 Thus will I magnify myself, and sanctify myself; and I will be known in the eyes of many nations, and they shall know that I am the Lord.*

Ezekiel 38 is thus concluded. We will now move into Ezekiel 39. Since I have yet to post the text of that chapter, I will do so now. Afterward, we will pick up where we left off in the sequence of events and see how Ezekiel 39 details the fallout of this battle. I will also discuss where this conflict will take place and what the ultimate outcome of it is, as it relates to the End Times Timeline.

Ezekiel 39:1-29 (KJV)[25]

1 Therefore, thou son of man, prophesy against Gog, and say, Thus saith the Lord God; Behold, I am against thee, O Gog, the chief prince of Meshech and Tubal: 2 And I will turn thee back, and leave but the sixth part of thee, and will cause thee to come up from the north parts, and will bring thee upon the mountains of Israel: 3 And I will smite thy bow out of thy left hand, and will cause thine arrows to fall out of thy right hand. 4 Thou shalt fall upon the mountains of Israel, thou, and all thy bands, and the people that is with thee: I will give thee unto the ravenous birds of every sort, and to the beasts of the field to be devoured. 5 Thou shalt fall upon the open field: for I have spoken it, saith the Lord God. 6 And I will send a fire on Magog, and among them that dwell carelessly in the isles: and they shall know that I am the Lord. 7 So will I make my holy name known in the midst of my people Israel; and I will not let them pollute my holy name any more: and the heathen shall know that I am the Lord, the Holy One in Israel. 8 Behold, it is come, and it is done, saith the Lord God; this is the day whereof I have spoken. 9 And they that dwell in the cities of Israel shall go forth, and shall set on fire and burn the weapons, both the shields and the bucklers, the bows and the arrows, and the handstaves, and the spears, and they shall burn them with fire seven years: 10 So that they shall take no wood out of the field, neither cut down any out of the forests; for they shall burn the weapons with fire: and they shall spoil those that spoiled them, and rob those that robbed them, saith the Lord God. 11 And it shall come to pass in that day, that I will give unto Gog a place there of graves in Israel, the valley of the passengers on the east of the sea: and it shall stop the noses of the passengers: and there shall they bury Gog and all his multitude: and they shall call it The valley of Hamongog. 12 And seven months shall the house of Israel be burying of them, that they may cleanse the land. 13 Yea, all the people of the land shall bury them; and it shall be to them a renown the day that I shall be glorified, saith the Lord God. 14 And they shall sever out men of continual employment, passing through the land to bury with the passengers those that remain upon the face of the earth, to cleanse it: after the end of seven months shall they search. 15 And the passengers that pass through the land, when any seeth a man's bone, then shall he set up a sign by it, till the buriers have buried it in the valley of Hamongog. 16 And also the name of the city shall be Hamonah. Thus shall they cleanse the land. 17 And, thou son of man, thus saith the Lord God; Speak unto every feathered fowl, and to every beast of the field, Assemble yourselves, and come; gather yourselves on every side to my sacrifice that I do sacrifice for you, even a great sacrifice upon the mountains of Israel, that ye may eat flesh, and drink blood. 18 Ye shall eat the flesh of the mighty, and drink the blood of the princes of the earth, of rams, of lambs, and of goats, of bullocks, all of them fatlings of Bashan. 19 And ye shall eat fat till ye be full, and drink blood till ye be drunken, of my sacrifice which I have sacrificed for you. 20 Thus ye shall be filled at my table with horses and chariots, with mighty men, and with all men of war, saith the Lord God. 21 And I will set my glory among the heathen, and all the heathen shall see my judgment that I have executed, and my hand that I have laid upon them. 22 So the house of Israel shall know that I am the Lord their God from that day and forward. 23 And the heathen shall know that the house of Israel went into captivity for their iniquity: because they trespassed against me, therefore hid I my face from them, and gave them into the hand of their enemies: so fell they all by the sword. 24 According to their uncleanness and according to their transgressions have I done unto them, and hid my face from them. 25 Therefore thus saith the Lord God; Now will I bring again the captivity of Jacob, and have mercy upon the whole house of Israel, and will be jealous for my holy name; 26 After that they have borne their shame, and all their trespasses whereby they have trespassed against me, when they dwelt safely in their land, and none made them afraid. 27 When I have brought them again from the people, and gathered them out of their enemies' lands, and am sanctified in them in the sight of many nations; 28 Then shall they know that I am the Lord their God, which caused them to be led into captivity among the heathen: but I have gathered them unto their own land, and have left none of them any more there. 29 Neither will I hide my face any more from them: for I have poured out my spirit upon the house of Israel, saith the Lord God.

How God's Purpose is Accomplished - Ezekiel 39

In the first verses of Ezekiel 39, we have a restatement of God's purpose against Gog and of His judgment against Gog and Gog's armies.

> *1 Therefore, thou son of man, prophesy against Gog, and say, Thus saith the Lord God; Behold, I am against thee, O Gog, the chief prince of Meshech and Tubal: 2 And I will turn thee back, and leave but the sixth part of thee, and will cause thee to come up from the north parts, and will bring thee upon the mountains of Israel:*

I had mentioned there is a line of thought suggesting this conflict does not actually occur in Israel. The preceding verses clearly show such thinking is inaccurate. As was stated in Ezekiel 38, Ezekiel 39 also makes it clear this devastation will occur on the mountains of Israel. Again, this is a reference to Ezekiel 36 wherein the prophecy about Israel being gathered back into her land is specifically aimed at the desolate mountains which will be made fruitful.

The KJV is the only translation of the Bible, to my knowledge, which uses the verbiage shown in verse 2: *"and leave but the sixth part of thee"*. It appears to be a common misconception, perhaps stemming from using only a surface interpretation, that God will not actually destroy the entirety of Gog's army but will leave 1/6 of them alive. This, as we will see further supported from the text of the chapter, is incorrect.

According to Biblical commentaries, the verbiage *"and leave but the sixth part of thee"* is a reference to God leading Gog and Gog's armies about with a "hook of six teeth".[26] This is supported by the reference to the six ways in which the entirety of the army will be killed, as seen in Ezekiel 38:22 – with blood, pestilence, overflowing rain, great hailstones, fire, and brimstone. We also see from the following verses none of Gog's army will be left alive:

> *3 And I will smite thy bow out of thy left hand, and will cause thine arrows to fall out of thy right hand. 4 Thou shalt fall upon the mountains of Israel, thou, and all thy bands, and the people that is with thee: I will give thee unto the ravenous birds of every sort, and to the beasts of the field to be devoured. 5 Thou shalt fall upon the open field: for I have spoken it, saith the Lord God.*

Thus, it is clear the entirety of the army will be wiped out by the hand of God.

We will come back to the mention of the birds and the open field when we discuss where exactly this event may occur. Before we get there, verse 6 reminds us the original prophecy was not just against Gog, but also against the land of Magog. Recall Ezekiel 38:2:

> *2 Son of man, set thy face against Gog, the land of Magog, the chief prince of Meshech and Tubal, and prophesy against him,*

In Ezekiel 39:6, we see devastation will also be wrought on the land of Magog.

> *6 And I will send a fire on Magog, and among them that dwell carelessly in the isles: and they shall know that I am the* LORD.

The word "isles" is not a reference to islands, but rather to those who dwell in far-reaching places and consider themselves safe from the wrath of God. Hence, we see use of the word "carelessly". Ezekiel 39:6 contains the second occurrence of the word "carelessly" used within the context of the two chapters. The first was in Ezekiel 38:8, referring to the words "dwell safely".

> *8 After many days thou shalt be visited: in the latter years thou shalt come into the land that is brought back from the sword, and is gathered out of many people, against the mountains of Israel, which have been always waste: but it is brought forth out of the nations, and they shall* **dwell safely** *all of them.*

One of the fields of thought regarding the timing of this conflict suggests it will occur directly after a "peace treaty" is signed, therefore affording Israel the status of "dwelling safely", securely, or "carelessly" in her land. This viewpoint is typically held by those who would believe the Daniel 9:27 covenant to be a peace treaty, a view I do not share. In fact, Part Two of this study will break down the exact language contained in the 70th Week prophecy and determine what the covenant will truly be.

    As is evidenced by use of the word "carelessly" to describe both the inhabitants of Magog and Israel, we can ascertain a "peace treaty" is not necessary to consider one's self as "dwelling safely", securely, or "carelessly". Rather, the Hebrew word "betach" means the following: *"abstract, safety, both the fact (security) and the feeling (trust)."*[27] Israel is dwelling securely in her land, because the international community recognizes her right to be there. She dwells confidently in her land because she believes she has the capability to defend herself. The "peace treaty", anticipated to be made by the Antichrist, is not a precondition for the commencement of the Battle of Gog and Magog simply because Israel feels a measure of safety. Magog will feel the same measure of safety, and it is surely not the people group intended in Daniel 9:27. Rather, as we get further through the chapter, I will illustrate why the covenant occurring before this battle is not only unlikely, but it would be seemingly detrimental to God's purpose.

In the next verses of Ezekiel 39, we arrive again at the purposes for this conflict: for God to reveal Himself to the heathen nations and to elicit a response from Israel.

> *7 So will I make my holy name known in the midst of my people Israel; and I will not let them pollute my holy name any more: and the heathen shall know that I am the Lord, the Holy One in Israel. 8 Behold, it is come, and it is done, saith the Lord God; this is the day whereof I have spoken.*

Thus, in defeating Gog and Gog's armies on behalf of Israel, God will have begun to accomplish His purposes for bringing about the fulfillment of this prophecy.

What Will Israel's Role Be?

Other than being the object of Gog's "affection", Israel will not yet have had a role in this conflict. God will have singlehandedly defeated the entire enemy army without her assistance. However, after God has destroyed them all, Israel will be given her role. She will be on cleanup duty.

> *9 And they that dwell in the cities of Israel shall go forth, and shall set on fire and burn the weapons, both the shields and the bucklers, the bows and the arrows, and the handstaves, and the spears, and they shall burn them with fire seven years: 10 So that they shall take no wood out of the field, neither cut down any out of the forests; for they shall burn the weapons with fire: and they shall spoil those that spoiled them, and rob those that robbed them, saith the Lord God.*

Here we see the people of Israel being tasked with burning all the weapons of the enemy army for seven years. You may recall the army was described as a "cloud to cover the land". In Ezekiel 39:10, we are told there will be so many weapons to burn, Israel will not have to seek alternate fuel for the entire seven years. Furthermore, she will be given latitude to loot the armies which had attempted to loot her.

This period of weapons burning is another point of contention amongst prophecy teachers. I mentioned there are various viewpoints held within the prophecy community relating to the timing of this conflict. One such viewpoint suggests it will precede Daniel's 70th Week. I would agree. However, another viewpoint takes that position a bit further and suggests the conflict will occur a period of years before the start of the 70th Week, more specifically about three and a half years beforehand. This conclusion is drawn, because the seven-year period of weapons burning is inaccurately linked to the command given at the midpoint of the Week for Israel to flee after she sees the Abomination of Desolation.

> *Matthew 24:15 When ye therefore shall see the abomination of desolation, spoken of by Daniel the prophet, stand in the holy place, (whoso readeth, let him understand:) 16 Then let them which be in Judaea flee into the mountains: 17 Let him which is on the housetop not come down to take any thing out of his house: 18 Neither let him which is in the field return back to take his clothes. 19 And woe unto them that are with child, and to them that give suck in those days! 20 But pray ye that your flight be not in the winter, neither on the sabbath day: 21 For then shall be great tribulation, such as was not since the beginning of the world to this time, no, nor ever shall be. 22 And except those days should be shortened, there should no flesh be saved: but for the elect's sake those days shall be shortened.*[28]

The Olivet Discourse, as given by Jesus in Matthew 24, was spoken to the Jews. Conversely, as seen in Ezekiel 39:9, the command to burn the weapons is given to *"they that dwell in the cities of Israel"*. Ezekiel's directive is not specific to the Jews. Furthermore, we can see from other passages of Scripture not all the Jews will flee. I will reference two passages of Scripture specifically.

> *Revelation 12:14 And to the woman were given two wings of a great eagle, that she might fly into the wilderness, into her place, where she is nourished for a time, and times, and half a time, from the face of the serpent. 15 And the serpent cast out of his mouth water as a flood after the woman, that he might cause her to be carried away of the flood. 16 And the earth helped the woman, and the earth opened her mouth, and swallowed up the flood which the dragon cast out of his mouth. 17 And the dragon was wroth with the woman, and went to make war with the remnant of her seed, which keep*

the commandments of God, and have the testimony of Jesus Christ.[29]

We can see from the language used in Revelation 12:17 there will be Jews who do not flee. Satan is seen going to make war with them when he discovers he is unable to kill the fleeing remnant, which will be supernaturally protected by God. Furthermore, we see the same idea evidenced in Zechariah 13:9.

> *Zechariah 13:9 And I will bring the third part through the fire, and will refine them as silver is refined, and will try them as gold is tried: they shall call on my name, and I will hear them: I will say, It is my people: and they shall say, The LORD is my God.*[30]

While I do share the opinion that this conflict will occur prior to the start of Daniel's 70th Week, I do not share the opinion it will occur a period of years beforehand. I will explain my position in further detail as we work our way through Ezekiel 39. It will also be made abundantly clear by the timeline set forth in Part Five why this cannot be the case.

There is another viewpoint which links this conflict to Armageddon. While I won't go into great detail, I will point out notable differences. First, Ezekiel 38-39 is about invading Israel to take a spoil. It is not about meeting Jesus at His Second Coming to defeat Him, as is the purpose of Armageddon. We will walk through the events of the Second Coming more fully in Part Four of this study. Secondly, it is believed Armageddon will occur in the Valley of Megiddo, or the Kidron Valley. This is not the same battleground for Gog and Magog. We will see that momentarily. Furthermore, Gog leads the invasion against Israel in Ezekiel 38-39. Armageddon is led by the Antichrist. Lastly, there are differences with how the armies meet their respective ends. God will defeat the Ezekiel 38-39 army in six different ways: with blood, pestilence, overflowing rain, great hailstones, fire, and brimstone. Jesus will defeat the armies allied against Him at His Second Coming with the sword which proceeds out of His mouth.

Linking Ezekiel 38-39's Battle of Gog and Magog to any point in time after the start of the Week sees the weapons-burning ending at some point inside of the Millennial Kingdom. This theory does not work with key scriptures which refer to the fire reserved for the Day of Judgment, which will burn up the earth and the works therein. It should go without saying such fire would put an end to any weapons burning.

> *II Peter 3:10 But the day of the Lord will come as a thief in the night; in the which the heavens shall pass away with a great noise, and the elements shall melt with fervent heat, the earth also and the works that are therein shall be burned up.*[31]
>
> *Matthew 24:35 Heaven and earth shall pass away, but my words shall not pass away.*[32]

Seeing this to be the case, it really cannot fit within the scope of the prophecy to place the Battle of Gog and Magog and its subsequent weapons burning elsewhere than in alignment with the 70th Week. There is a very distinct reason they are both seven years. Having said that, let's continue with Ezekiel 39.

> *11 And it shall come to pass in that day, that I will give unto Gog a place there of graves in Israel, the valley of the passengers on the east of the sea: and it shall stop the noses of the passengers: and there shall they bury Gog and all his multitude: and they shall call it The valley of Hamongog. 12 And seven months shall the house of Israel be burying of them, that they may cleanse the land. 13 Yea, all the people of the land shall bury them; and it shall be to them a renown*

> *the day that I shall be glorified, saith the Lord God. 14 And they shall sever out men of continual employment, passing through the land to bury with the passengers those that remain upon the face of the earth, to cleanse it: after the end of seven months shall they search. 15 And the passengers that pass through the land, when any seeth a man's bone, then shall he set up a sign by it, till the buriers have buried it in the valley of Hamongog. 16 And also the name of the city shall be Hamonah. Thus shall they cleanse the land.*

In addition to burning weapons, Israel will also be tasked with burying the bodies of the dead. This will take her seven months to complete, and specific people will be set aside to complete the task. Furthermore, passersby will be given instruction to mark the bones they encounter so they can be buried.

> *"The extremest defilement, according to the Mosaic law, was caused by a dead body or by human bones. From this the land could only be purified by the burial of the last vestige of the host of Gog."*[33]

Where Will the Battle of Gog and Magog Occur?

We are told in Ezekiel 39:11 Gog and Gog's army will be given a resting place in the land of Israel. The specific location is mentioned twice in Ezekiel 39, with the first mention in verse 11 as being "east of the sea". There are different conjectures made about which sea is being referenced, the Dead Sea or the Sea of Galilee. The second mention of location is in verse 18, where Bashan is specifically called out.

Biblical Bashan is the modern-day Golan Heights. This area is, as verse 11 pointed out, east of both the Dead Sea and the Sea of Galilee. However, there is a bit more information given to help us narrow it down. The entire reference to "east of the sea" is *"the valley of the passengers east of the sea"*. This valley is linked to the area of Gilead, also written of in Ezekiel 47:18. From the Jamieson-Fausset-Brown Bible Commentary, we read the following:

> *"...those travelling on the high road, east of the Dead Sea, from Syria to Petra and Egypt. The publicity of the road would cause many to observe God's judgments, as the stench (as English Version translates) or the multitude of graves (as Henderson translates, "it shall stop the passengers") would arrest the attention of passers-by. Their grave would be close to that of their ancient prototypes, Sodom and Gomorrah in the Dead Sea, both alike being signal instances of God's judgments."*[34]

Thus, I would conjecture the location specified as "east of the sea" is more likely a reference to the Dead Sea. The language *"over the mountains"* is used multiple times to reference where Gog's attack will come from. We can see the mountains plainly on the map below. It also happens to be the area Moses was in when he overlooked the Promised Land just before he died, being denied entry therein. Furthermore, we see that area in ancient Israel was once inhabited by tribes of giants.

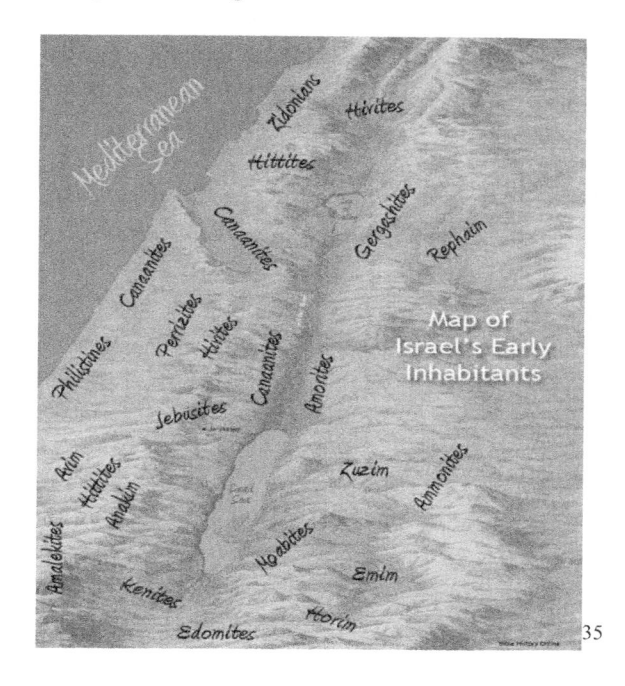

17 And, thou son of man, thus saith the Lord God; Speak unto every feathered fowl, and to every beast of the field, Assemble yourselves, and come; gather yourselves on every side to my sacrifice that I do sacrifice for you, even a great sacrifice upon the mountains of Israel, that ye may eat flesh, and drink blood. 18 Ye shall eat the flesh of the mighty, and drink the blood of the princes of the earth, of rams, of lambs, and of goats, of bullocks, all of them fatlings of Bashan. 19 And ye shall eat fat till ye be full, and drink blood till ye be drunken, of my sacrifice which I have sacrificed for you. 20 Thus ye shall be filled at my table with horses and chariots, with mighty men, and with all men of war, saith the Lord God.

If you're like me, you may have wondered why Israel is commanded to bury the bones. As we can see from the verses referenced above, the birds will be directed to feast on the flesh of the dead army and dead animals. There probably won't be much more than bones left to bury.

What isn't immediately obvious in the KJV is the reference to giants. In the Septuagint, giants are referenced twice within these verses. They read as follows:

> *Ezekiel 39:17 And you, son of man, say, This is what the Lord says: Say to every winged bird and to all the animals of the plain, Be gathered, and come; be gathered from all around the surrounding areas for my sacrifice that I have slaughtered for you, a great sacrifice upon the mountains of Israel, and you shall eat meat and drink blood. 18 You shall eat the flesh of giants and drink the blood of rulers of the earth, rams and calves and goats. And all the bull calves have been fattened. 19 And you shall eat fat unto satiety and drink blood unto drunkenness from my sacrifice that I have slaughtered for you. 20 And you shall be satisfied at my table: horse and rider and giant and every warrior, says the Lord.*[36]

Gog and Magog are celebrated as giants. The excerpt below regards the celebration of The Lord Mayor's Parade and the "patron-saints" of London.

> *"The 14ft-high wicker figures of the giants Gog and Magog are being spruced up for the Lord Mayor's procession, which they will lead in a few weeks' time. Sticklers insist that they should be called Magog and Corineus, placing their confidence in the 12th-century account by Geoffrey of Monmouth of the fight between those two heroic figures. But*

> *the City of London giants are carefully labelled Gog and Magog. The names are found in the Bible, though it is unforthcoming about their nature. "Son of man," says the prophet Ezekiel, "direct your face against Gog, of the land of Magog."[37]*

Lest one thinks the description of Gog and Magog as giants is fanciful, the Great Wall of China was originally called the Rampart of Gog and Magog. From the Benson Commentary:

> *"We find, Genesis 10:2, that the second son of Japhet was called Magog, but Ezekiel uses the word here as the name of the country of which Gog was prince: and Michaelis thinks that it denotes those vast regions to the north of India and China, which the Greeks called Scythia, and which we term Tartary. Houbigant also thinks that the prophet here means the Scythians, who are the descendants of Magog, the son of Japhet, and whose neighbours were the people of Rosh, Meshech, and Tubal; that is, the Russians, Muscovites, and Tibareni, or Cappadocians; and thus Theodoret and Josephus understand it. The Turks are generally allowed to be of Scythian origin. Scythopolis and Hierapolis, which cities the Scythians took when they overcame Syria, were ever after by the Syrians called Magog: see Plin, 50. 5. c. 23. The Arabs call the Chinese wall Sud Yagog et Magog, that is, the mud wall, or rampart of Gog and Magog."[38]*

This insight gives one pause to consider the additional ramifications of this conflict. The Great Wall of China was built to keep out hordes of giants, led by Gog and Magog. However, Israel doesn't have walls like the Great Wall to keep giants out, which is likely why Ezekiel 38 refers to Israel as "the land of unwalled villages". It's enlightening to consider there will not only be giants involved in Ezekiel 38-39, but God will use His defeat of those giants to glorify

Himself. We see such references to God glorifying Himself in the next verses of Ezekiel 39.

> *21 And I will set my glory among the heathen, and all the heathen shall see my judgment that I have executed, and my hand that I have laid upon them. 22 So the house of Israel shall know that I am the Lord their God from that day and forward.*

When Will the Battle of Gog and Magog Occur?

We have briefly discussed what God's purposes are regarding the Battle of Gog and Magog, as well as how He will accomplish them. However, the final verses of Ezekiel 39 discuss the fulfillment of His purpose toward Israel in far greater detail. After all, it is Israel who is in view in Daniel's 70th Week.

Lest we think the church is considered at all in this Ezekiel 38-39 prophecy, we must remember one very important point: there are only two groups referenced regarding God's purposes, and both are unbelievers. Only the heathen and Israel are mentioned. God has nothing to prove to the church, nor does He have any reason to show Himself to the church. We already believe in Him.

II Corinthians 5:7 (For we walk by faith, not by sight:)[39]

It is because the unbelieving world, and specifically Israel, does not walk by faith that His overt actions are necessary to precipitate a paradigm shift.

I have already mentioned wrath is not something the church age is subject to. More specifically, the wrath of God is not something His church members are subject to. It is one of the things our presence on this earth is restraining. Jesus taught this concept in Matthew 12, although it was in a different context. He said a house divided against itself cannot stand. God will not pour out His wrath while those who are indwelled by His Spirit are upon this earth. In fact, it is for that very reason we are not subject to judgment; because He dwells within us. Through the person of Jesus Christ, the wrath of God was already satisfied. Thus, we who are "in Christ" have been granted the grace to forgo the judgment our sins should require. God will remove the righteous before judging the wicked, just like He did with Lot.

Let's continue with Ezekiel 39. Verse 22 is especially important in this context.

> *21 And I will set my glory among the heathen, and all the heathen shall see my judgment that I have executed, and my hand that I have laid upon them. 22 So the house of Israel shall know that I am the Lord their God from that day and forward.*

Through His overt actions on behalf of His people, Israel, God will seek to draw them back into a covenant relationship with Him. This covenant will not immediately be the New Covenant, as that requires belief in the Lord Jesus Christ. Rather, He will begin to draw Israel back via the Old Covenant. We see this concept written of in Revelation 11:1-2 and Daniel 9:27. The first orders of business in the 70th Week will be the rebuilding of the temple and the reinstitution of the sacrificial system. The Old Covenant, which requires strict adherence to the Mosaic Law, cannot properly be followed without those things.

> *Revelation 11:1 And there was given me a reed like unto a rod: and the angel stood, saying, Rise, and measure the temple of God, and the altar, and them that worship therein. 2 But the court which is without the temple leave out, and measure it not; for it is given unto the Gentiles: and the holy city shall they tread under foot forty and two months.*[40]

We further know from Daniel 9:27, the reestablishment of said activities will take precedence at the start of the Week. The cessation of the sacrificial system and offerings at the midpoint of the Week presupposes the prior implementation of said systems. If they do not exist, they cannot be stopped. Thus, we know they will resume prior to the midpoint of the Week.

> *Daniel 9:27 And he shall confirm the covenant with many for one week: and in the midst of the week he shall cause the sacrifice and the oblation to cease, and for the overspreading of abominations he shall make it desolate, even until the consummation, and that determined shall be poured upon the desolate.*

In Matthew 24:15-22, Jesus gave the command to Israel to flee at the midpoint of the Week, when they see the Abomination of Desolation. This flight will allow a remnant of Israel to be spared from the events of the second half of the Week.

> *Matthew 24:15 When ye therefore shall see the abomination of desolation, spoken of by Daniel the prophet, stand in the holy place, (whoso readeth, let him understand:) 16 Then let them which be in Judaea flee into the mountains: 17 Let him which is on the housetop not come down to take any thing out of his house: 18 Neither let him which is in the field return back to take his clothes. 19 And woe unto them that are with child, and to them that give suck in those days! 20 But pray ye that your flight be not in the winter, neither on the sabbath day: 21 For then shall be great tribulation, such as was not since the beginning of the world to this time, no, nor ever shall be. 22 And except those days should be shortened, there should no flesh be saved: but for the elect's sake those days shall be shortened.*

It will not be until the end of the Week that Israel will be brought into a New Covenant relationship with her real Messiah, Jesus Christ. National redemption of Israel will occur at the end of the Week, and an Old Covenant relationship is insufficient for such redemption. She will simply understand at the midpoint of the Week, upon witnessing the Abomination of Desolation, the one she has been calling her messiah is not actually her Messiah. This will be addressed in much greater detail in Part Two of this study. For now, let's continue in Ezekiel 39.

> *23 And the heathen shall know that the house of Israel went into captivity for their iniquity: because they trespassed against me, therefore hid I my face from them, and gave them into the hand of their enemies: so fell they all by the sword. 24 According to their uncleanness and according to their transgressions have I done unto them, and hid my face from them. 25 Therefore thus saith the Lord God; Now will I bring again the captivity of Jacob, and have mercy upon the whole house of Israel, and will be jealous for my holy name; 26 After that they have borne their shame, and all their trespasses whereby they have trespassed against me, when they dwelt safely in their land, and none made them afraid.*

The verses above talk about Israel's rejection of her Messiah. Said rejection was the point at which Israel trespassed so badly God hid His face from her, even if only for a time. During the time His face has been hidden from Israel, it has been directed at the church. We see this written about in Romans 11.

> *Romans 11:15 For if the casting away of them be the reconciling of the world, what shall the receiving of them be, but life from the dead? 16 For if the firstfruit be holy, the lump is also holy: and if the root be holy, so are the branches. 17 And if some of the branches be broken off, and thou, being a wild olive tree, wert grafted in among them, and with them partakest of the root and fatness of the olive tree; 18 Boast not against the branches. But if thou boast, thou bearest not the root, but the root thee. 19 Thou wilt say then, The branches were broken off, that I might be grafted in. 20 Well; because of unbelief they were broken off, and thou standest by faith. Be not highminded, but fear: 21 For if God spared not the natural branches, take heed lest he also*

> *spare not thee. 22 Behold therefore the goodness and severity of God: on them which fell, severity; but toward thee, goodness, if thou continue in his goodness: otherwise thou also shalt be cut off. 23 And they also, if they abide not still in unbelief, shall be grafted in: for God is able to graft them in again. 24 For if thou wert cut out of the olive tree which is wild by nature, and wert grafted contrary to nature into a good olive tree: how much more shall these, which be the natural branches, be grafted into their own olive tree?*[41]

Romans 11:15 speaks of the very concept mentioned in Ezekiel 39:23, where Israel trespassed against God, and He hid His face from them. Thus, the dispensation called the "church age" began. In this nearly 2,000-year period, the Gospel of Jesus Christ which had been rejected by the Jews is currently being brought to and spread by the Gentiles.

Israel is the "natural branches" which were broken off. The "natural branches" will be grafted back into the "olive tree" at a later date, after Israel accepts Jesus as her Messiah. However, acceptance of Jesus as her Messiah will not occur until just before His Second Coming, as referenced in Zechariah 12-13.

The "wild branches" represent the Gentiles who can be grafted into the "olive tree", or into the seed of Abraham, as co-heirs with Christ. The only requisite for such grafting in is partaking of the "root", or believing in the Lord Jesus Christ unto salvation.

> *Galatians 3:16 Now to Abraham and his seed were the promises made. He saith not, And to seeds, as of many; but as of one, And to thy seed, which is Christ. 17 And this I say, that the covenant, that was confirmed before of God in Christ, the law, which was four hundred and thirty years after, cannot disannul, that it should make the promise of none effect. 18 For if the inheritance be of the law, it is no*

more of promise: but God gave it to Abraham by promise. 19 Wherefore then serveth the law? It was added because of transgressions, till the seed should come to whom the promise was made; and it was ordained by angels in the hand of a mediator. 20 Now a mediator is not a mediator of one, but God is one. 21 Is the law then against the promises of God? God forbid: for if there had been a law given which could have given life, verily righteousness should have been by the law. 22 But the scripture hath concluded all under sin, that the promise by faith of Jesus Christ might be given to them that believe. 23 But before faith came, we were kept under the law, shut up unto the faith which should afterwards be revealed. 24 Wherefore the law was our schoolmaster to bring us unto Christ, that we might be justified by faith. 25 But after that faith is come, we are no longer under a schoolmaster. 26 For ye are all the children of God by faith in Christ Jesus. [42]

Romans 11:25 speaks of the time when the dispensational change will occur, as also mentioned in Ezekiel 39. This dispensational change involves God removing the church via the rapture and turning His face back to Israel.

> *Romans 11:25 For I would not, brethren, that ye should be ignorant of this mystery, lest ye should be wise in your own conceits; that blindness in part is happened to Israel, until the fulness of the Gentiles be come in.* [43]

Ezekiel 39 says the following:

> *27 When I have brought them again from the people, and gathered them out of their enemies' lands, and am sanctified in them in the sight of many nations; 28 Then shall they know that I am the Lord their God, which caused them to be led into captivity among the heathen: but I have gathered them*

unto their own land, and have left none of them any more there. 29 Neither will I hide my face any more from them: for I have poured out my spirit upon the house of Israel, saith the Lord God.

Ezekiel 39:27 refers to the course of events documented in Ezekiel 36-39. Israel will have been gathered out of the nations and back into her land. Then, she will be sanctified, or set apart, in the sight of many nations through God's actions on her behalf regarding the Battle of Gog and Magog. After the fulfillment of those prophecies, God will stop hiding His face from Israel. Based on what we read in Romans 11, it is clear the church must be removed for this shift to occur. It also appears from the relation of Romans 11 to Ezekiel 39 that the rapture of the church may very well have something to do with the Battle of Gog and Magog.

God has two options for directing His focus: to Israel or to the church. If His focus was removed from Israel to be placed on the church, then it would stand to reason His focus will only return to Israel if focus on the church is no longer an option. Even so, His focus was only removed from Israel due to her trespass against Him. The church cannot trespass against Him, because He lives in us. We can never do what Israel did to lose His focus, which is to say, reject His Messiah. Therefore, He must physically remove us so we are no longer the object of His focus.

Please do not misunderstand my point and think I am suggesting God has limitations; that He cannot deal with two people groups at once. I am not suggesting He cannot do that. I am suggesting He <u>will not</u> do that. This principle is the very foundation of dispensationalism. We realize the church and Israel are different. We realize God does not deal with them in the same way. We realize God does not deal with them at the same time.

The presence of the church is not only keeping His focus hidden from Israel, but it is also keeping His wrath restrained, like I mentioned earlier. Perhaps equally as important, it is only the presence of the Holy Spirit-indwelled church that is keeping the time of the Antichrist restrained.

> *II Thessalonians 2:6 And now ye know what withholdeth that he might be revealed in his time. 7 For the mystery of iniquity doth already work: only he who now letteth will let, until he be taken out of the way. 8 And then shall that Wicked be revealed, whom the Lord shall consume with the spirit of his mouth, and shall destroy with the brightness of his coming: 9 Even him, whose coming is after the working of Satan with all power and signs and lying wonders, 10 And with all deceivableness of unrighteousness in them that perish; because they received not the love of the truth, that they might be saved. 11 And for this cause God shall send them strong delusion, that they should believe a lie: 12 That they all might be damned who believed not the truth, but had pleasure in unrighteousness.*[44]

We know from Daniel 9:27, the Antichrist, also called "that Wicked" in II Thessalonians 2:8, is the one who will confirm the covenant with many for one week. This supports the proximity of the rapture of the church to the events of Ezekiel 38-39 and the subsequent revelation of the Antichrist. This false Christ will ride the coattails of God's victory and help Israel reestablish her covenant (Old Covenant) relationship with God. Jack Kelley wrote the following on his website, www.gracethrufaith.com:

> *"This is one of the reasons why many scholars believe the Battle of Ezekiel 38 inaugurates the 70th Week of Daniel rather than taking place at its end. During the Great Tribulation (the last half of Daniel's 70th week) God's evangelistic effort will be to bring His people into a New*

Covenant relationship to save them. But Gabriel told Daniel a Temple would be rebuilt early in the 70th week, meaning that the Jews would first return to Him through the Old Covenant. The Temple has to be in place before the middle of the week to be desecrated by the anti-Christ (Daniel 9:27 and 2 Thes 2:4) kicking off the Great Tribulation.

Daniel's prophecy also implies that the anti-Christ will be involved in getting permission for Israel to build the Temple. This means that the Battle of Ezekiel 38 prepares the world for his entrance.

And finally the Battle of Ezekiel 38, having turned God's focus back to Israel, means the Age of the Church has ended. And the event that ends the Church Age is the Rapture. For that reason, the Rapture has to happen before or no later than during Ezekiel's battle."[45]

Final Thoughts

Based on all of the information presented, it is my belief the rapture of the church will likely occur near, or even during, Ezekiel 38-39's prophesied Battle of Gog and Magog. The removal of the church will facilitate God's overt actions on behalf of unbelieving Israel to not only draw her back into a covenant relationship with Him, but to remove the restraint on the time of the Antichrist. This series of events will bring about the fulfillment of Daniel 9:27 and the remainder of end times Bible prophecy.

Before I conclude Part One of the End Times Timeline, I need to come back to one statement I made earlier. I mentioned how placing the Battle of Gog and Magog after the start of the Week is seemingly detrimental to God's purpose. If we were to place the Battle within the Week, and if we account for the presence of any number of supernatural beings on earth during the Week, not the least of whom will be the Antichrist, False Prophet, and the two witnesses, there is no way to ensure the entire world will absolutely know for sure it was God who acted in defense of Israel. However, we see from Ezekiel 38-39 that the entire world will absolutely know for sure it was God who acted in defense of Israel.

God will not share the glory of His victory on behalf of Israel with anyone else. The only way to ensure He doesn't have to share it is to ensure there is no other presence on earth to whom His victory could be attributed. Since the Antichrist, False Prophet, and two witnesses will all have supernatural powers in their own rights, the Battle of Gog and Magog must then take place before any of them arrive.

PART TWO: The Daniel 9:27 Covenant

An Overview of the 70 Weeks

In Part Two of the End Times Timeline, I will break down the entirety of Daniel 9:27, the prophecy of the 70th Week. I will go through various words used and explain in as much detail as possible what they mean. I will also break down the timing of the events prophesied to occur, the last of which will be the lead-in to Part Three - The Feasts of the Lord. It is my hope by the time I'm done explaining the components of this verse, you will have a better understanding of the timeline of events Daniel 9:27 lays out. Having said that, let's get started.

To fully understand the covenant which will begin the 70th Week, we need to give ourselves context. To understand the 70th Week, we must understand the first 69 Weeks. If you read Part One, some of this may be redundant. However, I need to explain everything fully for those who may not have. The verses below detail the entire prophecy given to Daniel regarding the end times.

> *Daniel 9:20 And whiles I was speaking, and praying, and confessing my sin and the sin of my people Israel, and presenting my supplication before the LORD my God for the holy mountain of my God; 21 Yea, whiles I was speaking in prayer, even the man Gabriel, whom I had seen in the vision at the beginning, being caused to fly swiftly, touched me about the time of the evening oblation. 22 And he informed me, and talked with me, and said, O Daniel, I am now come forth to give thee skill and understanding. 23 At the beginning of thy supplications the commandment came forth, and I am come to shew thee; for thou art greatly beloved: therefore understand the matter, and consider the vision. 24 Seventy weeks are determined upon thy people and upon thy holy city, to finish the transgression, and to make an end of sins, and to make reconciliation for iniquity, and to bring in everlasting righteousness, and to seal up the vision and*

> *prophecy, and to anoint the most Holy. 25 Know therefore and understand, that from the going forth of the commandment to restore and to build Jerusalem unto the Messiah the Prince shall be seven weeks, and threescore and two weeks: the street shall be built again, and the wall, even in troublous times. 26 And after threescore and two weeks shall Messiah be cut off, but not for himself: and the people of the prince that shall come shall destroy the city and the sanctuary; and the end thereof shall be with a flood, and unto the end of the war desolations are determined. 27 And he shall confirm the covenant with many for one week: and in the midst of the week he shall cause the sacrifice and the oblation to cease, and for the overspreading of abominations he shall make it desolate, even until the consummation, and that determined shall be poured upon the desolate.*[46]

The first 69 Weeks of years have already been fulfilled. The decree to restore and rebuild Jerusalem was given by Artaxerxes on March 14, 445 B.C. From there, a day count of 173,880 days ends us up at Palm Sunday, April 6, 32 A.D.[47]

7 Weeks x 7 years per Week x 360 days per year = 17,640 days
62 Weeks x 7 years per Week x 360 days per year = 156,240 days

17,640 + 156,240 = 173,880 days in 69 Weeks

It was at the end of that very day count, on Palm Sunday, Jesus rode into Jerusalem on a donkey and presented Himself as the Lamb of God who would be sacrificed on Passover, four days later.

> *Matthew 21:5 Tell ye the daughter of Sion, Behold, thy King cometh unto thee, meek, and sitting upon an ass, and a colt the foal of an ass. 6 And the disciples went, and did as Jesus commanded them, 7 And brought the ass, and the colt, and put on them their clothes, and they set him thereon. 8 And a*

> *very great multitude spread their garments in the way; others cut down branches from the trees, and strawed them in the way. 9 And the multitudes that went before, and that followed, cried, saying, Hosanna to the son of David: Blessed is he that cometh in the name of the Lord; Hosanna in the highest. 10 And when he was come into Jerusalem, all the city was moved, saying, Who is this? 11 And the multitude said, This is Jesus the prophet of Nazareth of Galilee.*[48]

Daniel 9:26 tells us after the conclusion of the first 69 Weeks, Messiah would be "cut off", or killed, but not for Himself. Rather, He laid down His life for us, taking upon Himself the sins of the world. Thus, the New Covenant was established, and the "age of grace", also referred to as the church age, was born. In the stopping of the progression of those Weeks of years, we realize quickly one final Week of years remains unfulfilled. The final Week is the focus of Daniel 9:27.

> *Daniel 9:27 And he shall confirm the covenant with many for one week: and in the midst of the week he shall cause the sacrifice and the oblation to cease, and for the overspreading of abominations he shall make it desolate, even until the consummation, and that determined shall be poured upon the desolate.*

It's important to point out the church had no part in the first 69 Weeks. This is because the church did not yet exist. The purpose of going through The Battle of Gog and Magog first was to establish the end of the church age prior to the commencement of the final Week. Just as the church had no part in the first 69 Weeks, it will also have no part in the 70th Week. I will illustrate this point further within the course of this study. I briefly referred to the benefits of dispensational theology in Part One. In my opinion, such theology is the cornerstone of studying end times prophecy.

The Beginning of the 70th Week

There are three specific points in time referenced in Daniel 9:27: the beginning of the Week, the middle of the Week, and the end of the Week. We will start at the beginning. I'll be referring to Daniel 9:27 multiple times throughout the course of this study, if for no other reason than so you can see the exact language used as we make our way through each facet of the verse.

> *Daniel 9:27 And he shall confirm the covenant with many for one week: and in the midst of the week he shall cause the sacrifice and the oblation to cease, and for the overspreading of abominations he shall make it desolate, even until the consummation, and that determined shall be poured upon the desolate.*

Since we're starting at the beginning (a novel idea, I know…), let's segment the portion of the verse we'll be working with for the time being. I will essentially divide it into parts a, b, and c. Here is part "a":

> *Daniel 9:27 And he shall confirm the covenant with many for one week:*

The bulk of Part Two will be spent dissecting the information given in those words. We have already established the meaning of "one week". It refers to a final, yet unfulfilled period of seven years also called a "shabua". This Week of years will be just as the first 69 Weeks of years were, which is to say they will be comprised of 360-day years as understood of the ancient Hebrew calendar. The day counts will be supported when we move into various parts of Revelation concerning the events in the "midst of the week", or part "b" of Daniel 9:27. However, that isn't for just yet. Let's continue by addressing who the "he" being referenced in Daniel 9:27 is.

Who is "He"?

Daniel 9:26 gives us the answer to this question.

> *26 And after threescore and two weeks shall Messiah be cut off, but not for himself: and the people of <u>the prince that shall come</u> shall destroy the city and the sanctuary; and the end thereof shall be with a flood, and unto the end of the war desolations are determined.*

The "he" referenced in Daniel 9:27 is also named in verse 26 as the *"prince that shall come"*. We are told he will be linked in some way to the ancient Roman Empire, as it was Roman soldiers who destroyed the city and the sanctuary in 70 A.D.

There is debate within the prophecy community about whether this person will be a Muslim, indicating the final empire will be a revival of the Ottoman Empire or of the Caliphate. I disagree with that line of thinking, especially considering the Battle of Gog and Magog will have decimated a large amount of the fighting Muslim population. I won't go too far down that rabbit trail, but we are told in Daniel 2, with the discussion of the statue in Nebuchadnezzar's dream, the legs were made of iron. They symbolize the Roman Empire and its two branches. The 10 toes, indicative of the final empire, are also made of iron, but they are mixed with clay. It will be a revived Roman Empire, of sorts. Daniel 7 and 8 discuss the final ruler being descended from both the Roman and Greek empires. Please do not confuse the Roman Empire with Rome. They are not the same. Finally, Daniel 11:37 tells us this final ruler will not regard the "God of his fathers", which is to say, he will not regard the God of his forefathers: Abraham, Isaac, and Jacob. Thus, it is clear he will have some sort of tie to the 12 Tribes. We can understand from all of this he will not be Muslim.

While I prefer sticking as closely to the Biblical text as possible, I did find it pertinent to understand what the Jews are looking for in their messiah. I hope you all understand they will not be getting their real Messiah. Instead, they'll be getting one who comes in His place, or whom we refer to as the Antichrist. Let's look at some of their expectations.

The following, somewhat lengthy, excerpt is taken from an article on Chabad.org titled <u>"What is the Jewish Belief About Moshiach?"</u>[49]

What is the "End of Days"?

The term "End of Days" is taken from Numbers 24:14. This has always been taken as a reference to the messianic era. Here we shall explore—albeit briefly—the Jewish belief in the coming of Moshiach.

What does the word Moshiach mean?

Moshiach is the Hebrew word for "messiah." The word messiah in English means a savior or a "hoped-for deliverer." The word moshiach in Hebrew actually means "anointed." In Biblical Hebrew, the title moshiach was bestowed on somebody who had attained a position of nobility and greatness. For example, the high priest is referred to as the kohen ha-moshiach.

In Talmudic literature the title Moshiach, or Melech HaMoshiach (the King Messiah), is reserved for the Jewish leader who will redeem Israel in the End of Days.

What is the belief in Moshiach?

One of the principles of Jewish faith enumerated by Maimonides is that one day there will arise a <u>dynamic</u> Jewish leader, a direct descendant of the Davidic dynasty, who will rebuild the Temple in

Jerusalem, and gather Jews from all over the world and bring them back to the Land of Israel.

All the nations of the world will recognize Moshiach to be a world leader, and will accept his dominion. <u>*In the messianic era there will be world peace,*</u> *no more wars nor famine, and, in general, a high standard of living.*

All mankind will worship one G-d, and live a more spiritual and moral way of life. The Jewish nation will be preoccupied with learning Torah and fathoming its secrets.

The coming of Moshiach will complete G-d's purpose in creation: for man to make an abode for G-d in the lower worlds—that is, to reveal the inherent spirituality in the material world.

Is this not a utopian dream?

No! Judaism fervently believes that, with the correct leadership, humankind can and will change. The leadership quality of Moshiach means that through his dynamic personality and example, coupled with manifest humility, he will inspire all people to strive for good. He will transform a seemingly utopian dream into a reality. He will be recognized as a man of G-d, with greater leadership qualities than even Moses.

In today's society, many people are repulsed by the breakdown of ethical and moral standards. Life is cheap, crime is rampant, drug and alcohol abuse are on the increase, children have lost respect for their elders. At the same time, technology has advanced in quantum leaps. There is no doubt that today man has all the resources—if channeled correctly—to create a good standard of living for all mankind. He lacks only the social and political will. Moshiach will inspire all men to fulfill that aim.

Why the belief in a human messiah?

Some people believe that the world will "evolve" by itself into a messianic era without a human figurehead. Judaism rejects this belief. Human history has been dominated by empire builders greedy for power.

Others believe in Armageddon—that the world will self-destruct, either by nuclear war or by terrorism. Again, Judaism rejects this view.

Our prophets speak of the advent of a human leader, of a magnitude that the world has not yet experienced. His unique example and leadership will inspire mankind to change direction.

Where is Moshiach mentioned in the Scriptures?

The Scriptures are replete with messianic quotes. In Deuteronomy 30:1 Moses prophesies that, after the Jews have been scattered to the four corners of the earth, there will come a time when they will repent and return to Israel, where they will fulfill all the commandments of the Torah. The gentile prophet Balaam prophesies that this return will be led by Moshiach (see Numbers 24:17–20). Jacob refers to Moshiach by the name Shiloh (Genesis 49:10).

The prophets Isaiah, Jeremiah, Ezekiel, Amos, Joel and Hosea all refer to the messianic era. (For full references, the reader is referred to the book Moshiach by Rabbi Dr. J. I. Schochet.) It is interesting to note that the wall of the United Nations Building in New York is inscribed with the quote from Isaiah (11:6), "And the wolf shall lie with the lamb." Furthermore, it is clear from the prophets, when studied in their original Hebrew, that Moshiach is a Jewish concept, and his coming will entail a return to Torah law, firmly ruling out any "other" messianic belief.

What sort of leader will Moshiach be?

Moshiach will be a man who possesses extraordinary qualities. <u>He will be proficient in both the written and oral Torah traditions. He will incessantly campaign for Torah observance among Jews</u>, and observance of the seven universal Noahide laws by non-Jews. He will be scrupulously observant, and encourage the highest standards from others. He will defend religious principles and repair breaches in their observance. Above all, Moshiach will be heralded as a true Jewish king, a person who leads the way in the service of G-d, totally humble yet enormously inspiring.

When will Moshiach come?

Jews anticipate the arrival of Moshiach every day. Our prayers are full of requests to G-d to usher in the messianic era. Even at the gates of the gas chambers, many Jews sang "Ani Maamin"—I believe in the coming of Moshiach!

However, the Talmud states that there is a predestined time when Moshiach will come. If we are meritorious, he may come even before that predestined time. This "end of time" remains a mystery, yet the Talmud states that it will be before the Hebrew year 6000. (The Hebrew year at the date of this publication is 5772.)

What exactly will happen when Moshiach comes?

Maimonides states in his Mishneh Torah—a compendium of the entire halachic tradition—that <u>Moshiach will first rebuild the Temple and then gather in the exiles.</u> Jerusalem and the Temple will be the focus of divine worship, and "from Zion shall go forth Torah, and the word of the L-rd from Jerusalem."

The Sanhedrin—the supreme Jewish law court of 71 sages—will be re-established, and will decide on all matters of law. <u>At this time, all Jews will return to full Torah observance and practice.</u> It should be noted that in this present age of great assimilation and *emancipation, an unprecedented return of Jews to true Torah values has taken place. This "baal teshuvah" phenomenon is on the increase, and paves the way for a full return in the messianic era.*

Will miracles happen?

The Talmud discusses this question and again arrives at the conclusion that, if we are meritorious, the messianic redemption will be accompanied by miracles. However, the realization of the messianic dream, even if it takes place naturally, will be the greatest miracle.

According to some traditions, G-d Himself will rebuild the third Temple. According to others, it will be rebuilt by Moshiach; still others suggest a combination of the two opinions. Some suggest that there will be two distinct periods in the messianic era: first a non-miraculous period, leading into a second, miraculous period.

What will become of the world as we know it?

Initially, there will be no change in the world order, other than its readiness to accept messianic rule. All the nations of the world will strive to create a new world order, in which there will be no more wars or conflicts. Jealousy, hatred, greed and political strife (of the negative kind) will disappear, and all human beings will strive only for goodness, kindness and peace.

In the messianic era there will be great advances in technology, allowing a high standard of living. Food will be plentiful and cheap.

However, the focus of human aspiration will be the pursuit of the "knowledge of G-d." People will become less materialistic and more spiritual.

What are the "birthpangs" of Moshiach's arrival?

> *The Talmud describes the period immediately prior to the advent of Moshiach as one of great travail and turmoil. There will be a world recession, and governments will be controlled by despots. It is in this troubled setting that Moshiach will arrive.*
>
> *There is a tradition that a great war will take place, called the war of Gog and Magog, and there is much speculation as to the precise timing of this war in relation to Moshiach's arrival.*
>
> *There is a tradition that Elijah the Prophet will come to the world and announce the imminent arrival of Moshiach. However, according to other opinions, Moshiach may arrive unannounced. Elijah would then arrive to assist in the peace process. Some suggest that if the Moshiach arrives in his predestined time, then Elijah will announce his arrival; but if Moshiach comes suddenly, then Elijah will appear after Moshiach has come.*
>
> *As mentioned before, it is unclear as to exactly how these events will unfold. However, this uncertainty does not affect the general matter of Moshiach's arrival.*

If you did not have a clear understanding of what the Jews expect of their coming messiah, hopefully you now do. I underlined some points of interest in that article and will be going over each of them in greater detail. They are as follows:

- Dynamic
- In the messianic era, there will be world peace
- He will be proficient in both the written and oral Torah traditions. He will incessantly campaign for Torah observance among Jews
- Moshiach will first rebuild the Temple and then gather in the exiles
- At this time, all Jews will return to full Torah observance and practice
- "birthpangs"

- There is a tradition that a great war will take place, called the war of Gog and Magog, and there is much speculation as to the precise timing of this war in relation to Moshiach's arrival
- Elijah would then arrive to assist in the peace process

We can conclude the "he" who will be confirming the covenant and kicking off the 70th Week is the Antichrist since we know it will not be the true Christ. In Part One, I addressed his arrival in proximity to the Battle of Gog and Magog. The Jews also believe this to be the case, as is illustrated by the following point:

- There is a tradition that a great war will take place, called the war of Gog and Magog, and there is much speculation as to the precise timing of this war in relation to Moshiach's arrival.

What Does It Mean to "Confirm"?

The next part of Daniel 9:27 is the "confirmation of the covenant". There are two important principles in play within that phrase: what it means to "confirm" and what "the covenant" is a reference to. I'll begin with what the word "confirm" means.

The word "confirm" is the Hebrew word "gâbar" which means to *"to prevail, have strength, be strong, be powerful, be mighty, be great"*.[50] "Gâbar" is a verb. The subject of this verb is "he". The covenant is simply what is being confirmed by the Antichrist's show of strength, power, or might.

When we do a word study of Hebrew to Greek, we see the Hebrew word "gâbar" is the same as the Greek word "dynamóō"[51] (G1412). A quick search for the number of times "dynamóō" is used in the New Testament, as well as the verses wherein it is used, tells us this word is only used once in the entire New Testament.[52] Thus, we need to visit that verse to understand its context.

> *Colossians 1:10 That ye might walk worthy of the Lord unto all pleasing, being fruitful in every good work, and increasing in the knowledge of God; 11* **Strengthened** [G1412] *with all might, according to his glorious power, unto all patience and longsuffering with joyfulness;*[53]

In Colossians 1:11, we see use of the word "dynamóō" where we see the word "strengthened". Used again in verb form, it is the act strengthening by "might". In Colossians, the might and power of the Lord are doing the strengthening. In Daniel 9:27, the Antichrist is the one "strengthening" based on some other might or power.

To understand this concept more fully, we need to look further into the Greek word for "might". It's almost identical to the Greek word for "strengthened". Let's view the phrase "strengthened with all might" in the Greek. It'll be a lot easier to see the link between "strengthened" and "might".

Strengthened	G1412	δυναμόω dynamoō
with	G1722	ἐν en
all	G3956	πᾶς pas
might	G1411	δύναμις dynamis	54

As you can see, "strengthened" and "might" come from the same root word. I went through all that to help you understand the "confirming" the Antichrist does of the covenant is merely putting "strength" behind it. The more important question is, where does he get the power or "might" needed to provide said "strength"?

> *II Thessalonians 2:9 Even him, whose coming is after the working of Satan with all **power** ^{G1411} and signs and lying wonders,*[55]

The Antichrist gets the power or "might" with which he provides "strength" to the covenant from the working of Satan. We see this concept more fully supported in Revelation 13.

> *Revelation 13:4 And they worshipped the dragon which gave power unto the beast: and they worshipped the beast, saying, Who is like unto the beast? who is able to make war with him?*[56]

It is also interesting to note one of the sections of the article I posted from www.chabad.org mentioned the Jewish speculations on whether the arrival of their (false) messiah will include miracles. Indeed, it appears it will. This also addresses the previously underlined aspect of the Jewish expectations of their messiah:

- Dynamic (dynamóō, dynamis)

What is "the covenant"?

Some prophecy teachers believe the covenant will be forced upon Israel. Based on Scripture, this does not appear to be the case. We learn as much in John 5. To provide context for the statement Jesus made to prove their acceptance of the Antichrist and the covenant, we should understand the circumstances during which His statement was made.

> *John 5:1 After this there was a feast of the Jews; and Jesus went up to Jerusalem.*
>
> *14 Afterward Jesus findeth him in the temple, and said unto him, Behold, thou art made whole: sin no more, lest a worse thing come unto thee.*
>
> *18 Therefore the Jews sought the more to kill him, because he not only had broken the sabbath, but said also that God was his Father, making himself equal with God. 19 Then answered Jesus and said unto them, Verily, verily, I say unto you, The Son can do nothing of himself, but what he seeth the Father do: for what things soever he doeth, these also doeth the Son likewise. 20 For the Father loveth the Son, and sheweth him all things that himself doeth: and he will shew him greater works than these, that ye may marvel. 21 For as the Father raiseth up the dead, and quickeneth them; even so the Son quickeneth whom he will. 22 For the Father judgeth no man, but hath committed all judgment unto the Son: 23 That all men should honour the Son, even as they honour the Father. He that honoureth not the Son honoureth not the Father which hath sent him. 24 Verily, verily, I say unto you, He that heareth my word, and believeth on him that sent me, hath everlasting life, and shall not come into condemnation; but is passed from death unto life. 25 Verily, verily, I say unto you, The hour is coming, and now is, when the dead shall*

hear the voice of the Son of God: and they that hear shall live. 26 For as the Father hath life in himself; so hath he given to the Son to have life in himself; 27 And hath given him authority to execute judgment also, because he is the Son of man. 28 Marvel not at this: for the hour is coming, in the which all that are in the graves shall hear his voice, 29 And shall come forth; they that have done good, unto the resurrection of life; and they that have done evil, unto the resurrection of damnation. 30 I can of mine own self do nothing: as I hear, I judge: and my judgment is just; because I seek not mine own will, but the will of the Father which hath sent me. 31 If I bear witness of myself, my witness is not true. 32 There is another that beareth witness of me; and I know that the witness which he witnesseth of me is true. 33 Ye sent unto John, and he bare witness unto the truth. 34 But I receive not testimony from man: but these things I say, that ye might be saved. 35 He was a burning and a shining light: and ye were willing for a season to rejoice in his light. 36 But I have greater witness than that of John: for the works which the Father hath given me to finish, the same works that I do, bear witness of me, that the Father hath sent me. 37 And the Father himself, which hath sent me, hath borne witness of me. Ye have neither heard his voice at any time, nor seen his shape. 38 And ye have not his word abiding in you: for whom he hath sent, him ye believe not. 39 Search the scriptures; for in them ye think ye have eternal life: and they are they which testify of me. 40 And ye will not come to me, that ye might have life. 41 I receive not honour from men. 42 But I know you, that ye have not the love of God in you.

43 I am come in my Father's name, and ye receive me not: if another shall come in his own name, him ye will receive. 44 How can ye believe, which receive honour one of another, and seek not the honour that cometh from God only? 45 Do

> *not think that I will accuse you to the Father: there is one that accuseth you, even Moses, in whom ye trust.*
>
> *46 For had ye believed Moses, ye would have believed me; for he wrote of me. 47 But if ye believe not his writings, how shall ye believe my words?*[57]

There are a lot of verses there, so allow me to explain the main points. In the first verse of the chapter, we see there was a feast in Jerusalem. As such, the Jews would have been gathered in Jerusalem at the temple to celebrate it. Jesus was among them.

In the second section of verses, we see Jesus giving them the authority for His ministry. He plainly states He was sent by God to accomplish His purpose. He refers to Himself as the Son of God and walks the crowd, including both people and religious leaders, through the authority given Him by His Father. Such authority includes both the right to save and the right to judge at the end of the age. He then walks them through the fact His ministry was spoken of and taught about by John the Baptist. John bore witness to Jesus's coming and urged people to repent and believe. Thus, Jesus refers to John's ministry and explains how John's witness lent credibility to Jesus's claims. Finally, He tells them the Scriptures they hold so dearly also bear witness of Him, if they would only search them to see such truth.

The final section of verses I included refers to their continued unbelief. Jesus warns them, people and religious leaders alike, even as they stand there in rejection of Him, the true Son of God sent to redeem them, there will come a day when they will accept someone who comes in his own name.

> *43 I am come in my Father's name, and ye receive me not: if another shall come in his own name, him ye will receive.*

> *46 For had ye believed Moses, ye would have believed me; for he wrote of me. 47 But if ye believe not his writings, how shall ye believe my words?*

We can assuredly say, based on the claim Jesus makes, the covenant and the person who comes to confirm it will both be accepted by Israel. This claim is further supported by the fact that religious leaders currently wait in eager anticipation for the arrival of their messiah. It simply won't be the real Messiah they accept.

Many people believe the covenant will be a "peace treaty". Two points I referenced from the article on Chabad.org do address peace, although not as a treaty. Peace is simply an outcome of the arrival of their (false) messiah and his (false) prophet.

- In the messianic era, there will be world peace
- Elijah would then arrive to assist in the peace process

It is my understanding the idea the covenant will be a peace treaty largely stems from the verbiage contained in I Thessalonians 5:3.

> *I Thessalonians 5:3 For when they shall say, Peace and safety; then sudden destruction cometh upon them, as travail upon a woman with child; and they shall not escape.*[58]

This brings another point I underlined into focus:

- "birthpangs"

> *"Ancient Jewish eschatology taught that a seven year "time of trouble" would come upon the earth before the coming of the Messiah. During that time of trouble, the righteous would be resurrected and would enter the wedding chamber where they would be protected from the time of trouble. Today that*

seven year period is referred to, by Christians, as the Tribulation, and as Birth Pangs by the Jews."[59]

The period of time referred to as "birthpangs", or "travail upon a woman with child", is a reference to the 70th Week. The events which will lead into the final Week of years are regarded in I Thessalonians 5:3.

We must keep in mind the rapture was presented in I Thessalonians 4:13-18. In noting the sequential nature of the teachings in I Thessalonians, we can surmise the rapture to be pre-tribulational or pre-70th Week, since I Thessalonians 4 comes before I Thessalonians 5. The pre-tribulation rapture is also supported in II Thessalonians 2:6-8, as well as in the order of events from Revelation 4:1, Revelation 6:1-2, and Revelation 13. I will get to those in a bit. For now, let's go back to the "peace" aspect.

I Thessalonians 5:3 refers to a very specific point in time wherein "they" (not we, because the church will be gone) will say, "Peace and safety". This corresponds to the arrival of the false messiah, who, as mentioned above, is expected to usher in an era of peace. When "they" accept the covenant confirmed by this false messiah, Daniel's 70th Week will commence. The "travail upon a woman with child", or "birthpangs", is the seven-year period which will then lead to the Second Coming of the real Messiah.

We see similar language used in Revelation 12 describing the process to bring forth the Messiah at His First Coming.

> *Revelation 12:1 And there appeared a great wonder in heaven; a woman clothed with the sun, and the moon under her feet, and upon her head a crown of twelve stars: 2 And she being with child cried, <u>travailing in birth</u>, and pained to be delivered.*[60]

We further note the sudden destruction in I Thessalonians 5:3, described as "travail" or "birthpangs", comes upon "them" (not us, because the church will be gone), and "they" (not we, because the church will be gone) shall not escape.

Thus, I Thessalonians 5:3 details the events which will start the 70th Week. This is to say, it details the arrival of the false messiah, heralding an age of peace, and the acceptance of the covenant. The Daniel 9:27 covenant is not, however, a peace treaty. We can understand this more fully when we look at the different types of Biblical covenants and classify it.

The Hebrew word for covenant is "běriyth".[61]

I. covenant, alliance, pledge
   A. between men
      i. treaty, alliance, league (man to man)
      ii. constitution, ordinance (monarch to subjects)
      iii. agreement, pledge (man to man)
      iv. alliance (of friendship)
      v. alliance (of marriage)
   B. between God and man
      i. alliance (of friendship)
      ii. covenant (divine ordinance with signs or pledges)

Since the Antichrist will be coming as a world leader, presumed by Israel to be sent by God, we can rule out a covenant "between men". Whether he comes as just a man or with supernatural powers is irrelevant in the scope of this determination. From what I have gone through so far in this study, especially considering II Thessalonians 2:9 which says, *"Even him, whose coming is after the working of Satan with all power and signs and lying wonders,"* the most accurate way to classify this covenant is not as an alliance or a treaty or an agreement. The most accurate way to classify the Daniel 9:27 covenant is as an ordinance, divine or otherwise, with signs and pledges. Thus, we can see a peace treaty is not in view.

If the covenant isn't a peace treaty, then what is it?

To delve into this further, I need to refer to statements I both made and quoted in Part One of this study. Here is the relevant text:

> "We know from Daniel 9:27 the Antichrist, also called "that Wicked" in II Thessalonians 2:8, is the one who will confirm the covenant with many for one week. This supports the proximity of the rapture of the church to the events of Ezekiel 38-39 and the subsequent revelation of the Antichrist. This false Christ will ride the coattails of God's victory and help Israel reestablish her covenant relationship with God.

> *Jack Kelley wrote the following on his website, www.gracethrufaith.com:*

> *"This is one of the reasons why many scholars believe the Battle of Ezekiel 38 inaugurates the 70th Week of Daniel rather than taking place at its end. During the Great Tribulation (the last half of Daniel's 70th week) God's evangelistic effort will be to bring His people into a New Covenant relationship to save them. But Gabriel told Daniel a Temple would be rebuilt early in the 70th week, meaning that the Jews would first return to Him through the Old Covenant. The Temple has to be in place before the middle of the week to be desecrated by the anti-Christ (Daniel 9:27 and 2 Thes 2:4) kicking off the Great Tribulation.*

> *Daniel's prophecy also implies that the anti-Christ will be involved in getting permission for Israel to build the Temple. This means that the Battle of Ezekiel 38 prepares the world for his entrance.*
>
> *And finally the Battle of Ezekiel 38, having turned God's focus back to Israel, means the Age of the Church has ended. And the event that ends the Church Age is the Rapture. For that reason the Rapture has to happen before or no later than during Ezekiel's battle."*[62]

Let's look at the final underlined points I took from the article on www.chabad.org.

- He will be proficient in both the written and oral Torah traditions. He will incessantly campaign for Torah observance among Jews
- Moshiach will first rebuild the Temple and then gather in the exiles
- At this time, all Jews will return to full Torah observance and practice

Israel's expectations align with what Jack Kelley alluded to: being brought back into an Old Covenant relationship with God. Observance of the Old Covenant and its Mosaic law, or the Torah, requires a temple and the reinstitution of the sacrificial system.

As the body of Christ, we know Jesus was the final sacrifice for sins, and after Him there is no other.

> *Hebrews 10:8 Above when he said, Sacrifice and offering and burnt offerings and offering for sin thou wouldest not, neither hadst pleasure therein; which are offered by the law; 9 Then said he, Lo, I come to do thy will, O God. He taketh away the first, that he may establish the second. 10 By the which will we are sanctified through the offering of the body of Jesus Christ once for all. 11 And every priest standeth daily ministering and offering oftentimes the same sacrifices,*

> *which can never take away sins: 12 But this man, after he had offered one sacrifice for sins for ever, sat down on the right hand of God; From henceforth expecting till his enemies be made his footstool. 14 For by one offering he hath perfected for ever them that are sanctified.[63]*

Israel, however, does not recognize this.

> *Hebrews 9:16 For where a testament is, there must also of necessity be the death of the testator. 17 For a testament is of force after men are dead: otherwise it is of no strength at all while the testator liveth. 18 Whereupon neither the first testament was dedicated without blood.[64]*

From the verses above, we understand a testament, also called a covenant, is of no force unless blood is shed for it. The New Covenant was dedicated with the blood shed by Jesus on the cross for the remission of our sins. The Old Covenant was dedicated with the blood of animals. Thus, we can see how the stopping of the sacrifices and offerings – the shedding of blood for the remission of sin – in the midst of the Week would cause the covenant to break. An Abomination of Desolation would not do that. Neither would the cessation of sacrifices break a peace treaty. The cessation of sacrifices and offerings would only break a covenant whereupon their presence is necessary, which is to say, in the Old Covenant. Isaiah 28 also talks about the covenant which will begin the 70th Week.

> *Isaiah 28:15 Because ye have said, We have made a covenant with death, and with hell are we at agreement; when the overflowing scourge shall pass through, it shall not come unto us: for we have made lies our refuge, and under falsehood have we hid ourselves: 16 Therefore thus saith the Lord GOD, Behold, I lay in Zion for a foundation a stone, a tried stone, a precious corner stone, a sure foundation: he*

> *that believeth shall not make haste. 17 Judgment also will I lay to the line, and righteousness to the plummet: and the hail shall sweep away the refuge of lies, and the waters shall overflow the hiding place. 18 And your covenant with death shall be disannulled, and your agreement with hell shall not stand; when the overflowing scourge shall pass through, then ye shall be trodden down by it. 19 From the time that it goeth forth it shall take you: for morning by morning shall it pass over, by day and by night: and it shall be a vexation only to understand the report.[65]*

A covenant with death is one which will not lead to life, meaning it will not include profession of faith in Jesus Christ. The "overflowing scourge" is synonymous with I Thessalonians 5:3's "sudden destruction". How do we know the Mosaic Law is being referenced in Isaiah 28? Because of how it is referred to after Christ is come.

> *Romans 8:2 For the law of the Spirit of life in Christ Jesus hath made me free from the law of sin and death.[66]*

> *I Corinthians 15:56 The sting of death is sin; and the strength of sin is the law.[67]*

Galatians 3 also explains this concept.

> *Galatians 3:24 Wherefore the law was our schoolmaster to bring us unto Christ, that we might be justified by faith. 25 But after that faith is come, we are no longer under a schoolmaster. 26 For ye are all the children of God by faith in Christ Jesus.[68]*

It stands to reason the Antichrist will do everything he can to keep any focus off the real Messiah, Jesus Christ. The institution of the Old Covenant will divert attention from the real covenant all need to partake of for salvation, which is the New Covenant. In his efforts to do this, the Antichrist will allow the Jews to have what they want until it is time for him to stop allowing it. I will get to that in just a bit. Before I do so, I need to point out where in Revelation the beginning of the Week is noted.

Revelation's Sequence of Events

From a dispensational viewpoint, we understand the rapture of the church is pictured in Revelation 4:1.

> *Revelation 4:1 After this I looked, and, behold, a door was opened in heaven: and the first voice which I heard was as it were of a trumpet talking with me; which said, Come up hither, and I will shew thee things which must be hereafter.*[69]

"Hereafter" is the beginning of the prophetic chapters in Revelation, since everything that follows has not yet occurred. We see this language used in Revelation 1:19 where we are told there are three parts to the vision John was given: what was, what is, and what shall be "hereafter". The age John was in at the time he was given the vision is the same age we are presently in: the church age. Revelation 2-3's seven letters to the seven churches are representative of this.

We would then, holding a pre-tribulational or pre-70th Week view of the rapture, expect to find the commencement of the Week in some chapter or verse after Revelation 4:1. Indeed, that is exactly what we find.

> *Revelation 6:1 And I saw when the Lamb opened one of the seals, and I heard, as it were the noise of thunder, one of the four beasts saying, Come and see. 2 And I saw, and behold a white horse: and he that sat on him had a bow; and a crown was given unto him: and he went forth conquering, and to conquer.*

The rider on the white horse is the Antichrist. He is seen mirroring the image we are given in Revelation 19 of the Second Coming of the real Messiah.

> *Revelation 19:11 And I saw heaven opened, and behold a white horse; and he that sat upon him was called Faithful and True, and in righteousness he doth judge and make war. 12 His eyes were as a flame of fire, and on his head were many crowns; and he had a name written, that no man knew, but he himself. 13 And he was clothed with a vesture dipped in blood: and his name is called The Word of God. 14 And the armies which were in heaven followed him upon white horses, clothed in fine linen, white and clean.* [70]

We are further told the Antichrist will have a bow. The bow represents the Daniel 9:27 covenant. When looking for similar language in the Old Testament, we find a reference to a bow as a token or symbol of God's covenant in Genesis 9:13.

> *Genesis 9:13 I do set my bow in the cloud, and it shall be for a token of a covenant between me and the earth.* [71]

After the flood, God made a covenant stating He would never again destroy the world by water. He then sealed His covenant with a token, or a symbol, so when both He and the people on earth saw that symbol, all would be reminded of His promise.

The Hebrew word used in Genesis 9:13 for "bow" is "qesheth".[72] When translating the Hebrew to Greek, we see the Greek word for "bow" is "tóxon".[73] "Tóxon" is only used one time in the New Testament. It is found in Revelation 6:2 when describing the "bow" the Antichrist comes with. Thus, we can know for sure the bow being referenced in Revelation is indeed symbolic of the Daniel 9:27 covenant.

Please do not mistake me for suggesting the bow the Antichrist comes with will be a rainbow. Rather, I am only suggesting the language is symbolic in both Genesis and Revelation for their respective covenants. The Noahic Covenant is not in view in Revelation, nor is the rainbow, specifically. The verbiage about the "bow" as a symbol of a covenant is merely the same.

We further see from the placement of the rapture in Revelation 4:1 and the start of the final Week via confirmation of the covenant in Revelation 6:1-2, our pre-tribulational or pre-70th Week rapture parallels fit nicely with the sequence of events already referenced in I Thessalonians 4:13-18 (rapture) and I Thessalonians 5:3 (start of the 70th Week). There is another reference to the sequence of events in II Thessalonians 2:6-8 dealing with the necessary removal of restraint (Holy Spirit-indwelled church) prior to the revelation of the Antichrist, for the final Week to commence.

> *II Thessalonians 2:6 And now ye know what withholdeth that he might be revealed in his time. 7 For the mystery of iniquity doth already work: only he who now letteth will let, until he be taken out of the way. 8 And then shall that Wicked be revealed, whom the Lord shall consume with the spirit of his mouth, and shall destroy with the brightness of his coming:*[74]

Who Are the "Many"?

To round out part "a" of Daniel 9:27, we need to discuss who the "many" are with whom the covenant is confirmed. This will likely come as a surprise to few. The Hebrew word for "many" is "larabbim".[75] Essentially, the word means "many, many". The simplest explanation of who is intended here is found in the Jewish Encyclopedia entry titled <u>"Rabban", "Rabbi", and "Rab"</u>.[76]

> *"Hebrew term used as a title for those who are distinguished for learning, who are the authoritative teachers of the Law, and who are the appointed spiritual heads of the community. It is derived from the noun רב, which in Biblical Hebrew means "great" or "distinguished," and in post-Biblical Hebrew, "master" in opposition to "slave" (Suk. ii. 9; Giṭ. iv. 4) or "pupil" (Ab. i. 3).*
>
> *The title 'Rab' is Babylonian, and that of 'Rabbi' is Palestinian.*
>
> *The title 'Rabbi' is borne by the sages of Palestine, who were ordained there by the Sanhedrin in accordance with the custom handed down by the elders, and were denominated 'Rabbi,' and received authority to judge penal cases; while 'Rab' is the title of the Babylonian sages, who received their ordination in their colleges. The more ancient generations, however, which were far superior, had no such titles as 'Rabban,' 'Rabbi,' or 'Rab,' for either the Babylonian or Palestinian sages."*

Since Daniel was in Babylon during the time he received this prophecy, it is understandable he would use the Babylonian word "rab" when describing the religious leaders. The same word in Israel is "rabbi". Thus, we can identify that "larabbim", or the "many,

many" is a reference to the "teachers of the many", or to the religious leaders in Israel.

I referred to this same idea when discussing John 5. It was for this very reason I pointed out who was present during Jesus's dialogue about the nature of His purpose on earth and His revelation about being the Son of God. He was in Jerusalem at the temple for a feast. He would have been surrounded by the religious leaders of His time. We are told as much in the chapter where it is written they sought to kill Him not only for "working on the sabbath", but also for "making Himself equal with God".

Isaiah 28 also emphasizes the point about the covenant being confirmed with the religious leaders in Israel.

> *Isaiah 28:5 In that day shall the LORD of hosts be for a crown of glory, and for a diadem of beauty, unto the residue of his people, 6 And for a spirit of judgment to him that sitteth in judgment, and for strength to them that turn the battle to the gate. 7 But they also have erred through wine, and through strong drink are out of the way; the priest and the prophet have erred through strong drink, they are swallowed up of wine, they are out of the way through strong drink; they err in vision, they stumble in judgment.*
>
> *15 Because ye have said, We have made a covenant with death, and with hell are we at agreement; when the overflowing scourge shall pass through, it shall not come unto us: for we have made lies our refuge, and under falsehood have we hid ourselves:*[77]

The Barnes' Notes Biblical Commentary says the following:

> *"We are not to suppose that they had formally said this, but that their conduct was as if they had said it; they lived as*

securely as if they had entered into a compact with death not to destroy them, and with hell not to devour them. The figure is a very bold one, and is designed to express the extraordinary stupidity of the nation. It is most strikingly descriptive of the great mass of people. They are as little anxious about death and hell as if they had made a compact with the king of terrors and the prince of darkness not to destroy them. They are as little moved by the appeals of the gospel, by the alarms of God's providence, by the preaching of his word, and by all the demonstrations that they are exposed to eternal death, as though they had proved that there was no hell, or had entered into a solemn covenant that they should be unmolested."[78]

We now find our study of Daniel 9:27 part "a" complete. I hope I was thorough enough in my explanations so you understand all the components of the first part of the verse:

Daniel 9:27 And he shall confirm the covenant with many for one week:

The Middle of the 70th Week

The rest of Part Two will go relatively quickly since there is not much left to discuss regarding the remainder of Daniel 9:27. For the moment, though, we will focus on part "b".

> *Daniel 9:27 and in the midst of the week he shall cause the sacrifice and the oblation to cease, and for the overspreading of abominations he shall make it desolate,*

The midpoint of Daniel's 70th Week is characterized by two events: the cessation of sacrifices and offerings, and the Abomination of Desolation. We will begin with the cessation of the sacrifices and offerings.

"He shall cause the sacrifice and the oblation to cease"

I mentioned earlier how the confirmation of the Old Covenant would require a temple and reinstitution of the sacrificial system to adhere to the Mosaic Law. Not only does Israel believe the rebuilding of the temple will occur immediately after the arrival of her (false) messiah, Revelation 11 also tells us one will be built.

> *Revelation 11:1 And there was given me a reed like unto a rod: and the angel stood, saying, Rise, and measure the temple of God, and the altar, and them that worship therein. 2 But the court which is without the temple leave out, and measure it not; for it is given unto the Gentiles: and the holy city shall they tread under foot forty and two months.*[79]

It is at this temple the two witnesses will have the bulk of their ministry for the first 1260 days of the Week.

> *Revelation 11:3 And I will give power unto my two witnesses, and they shall prophesy a thousand two hundred and threescore days, clothed in sackcloth. 4 These are the two olive trees, and the two candlesticks standing before the God of the earth. 5 And if any man will hurt them, fire proceedeth out of their mouth, and devoureth their enemies: and if any man will hurt them, he must in this manner be killed. 6 These have power to shut heaven, that it rain not in the days of their prophecy: and have power over waters to turn them to blood, and to smite the earth with all plagues, as often as they will.*

Just as the first 69 Weeks were composed of 360-day years, so too will the 70th Week be. The Week will contain two halves, each consisting of 1260 days. We see these two periods of time referred to in Revelation 11-13 by the following: 1260 days; 42 months; and, a time, times, and half a time.

I also mentioned the covenant will not be broken by the Abomination of Desolation. Rather, it will be broken by the cessation of the sacrifice and oblation.

> *Hebrews 9:22 And almost all things are by the law purged with blood; and without shedding of blood is no remission.*[80]

If Israel can no longer offer sacrifices for the atonement of her sins, she will no longer have what she believes to be a viable Old Covenant relationship with the Lord. One line of thinking suggests the cutting off of the sacrifices and offerings and the Abomination of Desolation will not occur until the two witnesses are killed.

> *Revelation 11:7 And when they shall have finished their testimony, the beast that ascendeth out of the bottomless pit shall make war against them, and shall overcome them, and kill them. 8 And their dead bodies shall lie in the street of the great city, which spiritually is called Sodom and Egypt, where also our Lord was crucified. 9 And they of the people and kindreds and tongues and nations shall see their dead bodies three days and an half, and shall not suffer their dead bodies to be put in graves.*

After all, if they were alive and supernaturally empowered to stop the Antichrist (beast) from doing either thing, wouldn't they? I would think so. Thus, I would agree that neither the cessation of the sacrifices and offerings or the Abomination of Desolation will occur until after the two witnesses are killed. More to the point, I believe neither will likely occur until after they are resurrected, and the beast is angered that God subverted his actions in killing them.

> *Revelation 11:11 And after three days and an half the spirit of life from God entered into them, and they stood upon their feet; and great fear fell upon them which saw them. 12 And they heard a great voice from heaven saying unto them,*

Come up hither. And they ascended up to heaven in a cloud; and their enemies beheld them. 13 And the same hour was there a great earthquake, and the tenth part of the city fell, and in the earthquake were slain of men seven thousand: and the remnant were affrighted, and gave glory to the God of heaven. 14 The second woe is past; and, behold, the third woe cometh quickly. 15 And the seventh angel sounded; and there were great voices in heaven, saying, The kingdoms of this world are become the kingdoms of our Lord, and of his Christ; and he shall reign for ever and ever.

We now see the first half of the Week is over. Even so, Satan is not through with his plans for Israel yet. Revelation 12:10 picks up where the passage above in Revelation 11 ends, with the events of the 7th Trumpet judgment. Revelation 11 provides the earthly view. Revelation 12 provides the heavenly view. Below is Revelation 12's account of the events which occur in conjunction with the 7th Trumpet.

Revelation 12:10 And I heard a loud voice saying in heaven, Now is come salvation, and strength, and the kingdom of our God, and the power of his Christ: for the accuser of our brethren is cast down, which accused them before our God day and night. 11 And they overcame him by the blood of the Lamb, and by the word of their testimony; and they loved not their lives unto the death. 12 Therefore rejoice, ye heavens, and ye that dwell in them. Woe to the inhabiters of the earth and of the sea! for the devil is come down unto you, having great wrath, because he knoweth that he hath but a short time. 13 And when the dragon saw that he was cast unto the earth, he persecuted the woman which brought forth the man child. 14 And to the woman were given two wings of a great eagle, that she might fly into the wilderness, into her place, where she is nourished for a time, and times, and half a time, from the face of the serpent. 15 And the serpent cast out of

> *his mouth water as a flood after the woman, that he might cause her to be carried away of the flood. 16 And the earth helped the woman, and the earth opened her mouth, and swallowed up the flood which the dragon cast out of his mouth. 17 And the dragon was wroth with the woman, and went to make war with the remnant of her seed, which keep the commandments of God, and have the testimony of Jesus Christ.*[81]

It is interesting to note the events of the midpoint of the Week which correspond to the flight of the remnant bring to remembrance the events of the exodus. The remnant will be chased by Satan with the intent to destroy them, just like Pharaoh and his army chased the Israelites with similar intent. And just as God supernaturally protected the Israelites during the exodus, He will also supernaturally protect the fleeing remnant in Revelation 12. Verse 14 calls this being *"given two wings of a great eagle"*. Compare to Exodus 19.

> *Exodus 19:3 And Moses went up unto God, and the LORD called unto him out of the mountain, saying, Thus shalt thou say to the house of Jacob, and tell the children of Israel; 4 Ye have seen what I did unto the Egyptians, and how I bare you on eagles' wings, and brought you unto myself.*[82]

"And for the overspreading of abominations he shall make it desolate"

It is pertinent to point out the flight of the remnant immediately proceeds the Abomination of Desolation, the second of two events which occur at the midpoint of the Week.

> *Matthew 24:15 When ye therefore shall see the abomination of desolation, spoken of by Daniel the prophet, stand in the holy place, (whoso readeth, let him understand:) 16 Then let them which be in Judaea flee into the mountains: 17 Let him which is on the housetop not come down to take any thing out of his house: 18 Neither let him which is in the field return back to take his clothes. 19 And woe unto them that are with child, and to them that give suck in those days! 20 But pray ye that your flight be not in the winter, neither on the sabbath day: 21 For then shall be great tribulation, such as was not since the beginning of the world to this time, no, nor ever shall be. 22 And except those days should be shortened, there should no flesh be saved: but for the elect's sake those days shall be shortened.*[83]

Matthew 24:22 is often left out of the section of verses quoted regarding the flight of the remnant at the midpoint of the Week. However, it is important to place verse 22 in context with the rest of the passage to illustrate the importance of them fleeing immediately. Revelation 12:17 tells us when Satan is unsuccessful in his attempt to destroy them, he becomes *"wroth with the woman, and went to make war with the remnant of her seed"*. If a remnant of Jews does not flee, the whole of her will be wiped out. We can then infer there would be no Israel left to call upon Jesus for salvation, and thus, no Second Coming of Jesus Christ.

> *Matthew 23:39 For I say unto you, Ye shall not see me henceforth, till ye shall say, Blessed is he that cometh in the name of the Lord.*[84]

A remnant must be preserved. Thus, a remnant will be preserved.

But what is this Abomination of Desolation which sends Israel fleeing? Will it be the sacrifice of an unclean animal on the altar? Or a statue of a pagan god? Let's look at what the midpoint of the Week will look like, according to Revelation, Daniel, and II Thessalonians, and see if we can decipher what the Abomination of Desolation will be.

> *Revelation 13:4 And they worshipped the dragon which gave power unto the beast: and they <u>worshipped the beast</u>, saying, Who is like unto the beast? who is able to make war with him? 5 And there was given unto him a mouth speaking great things and blasphemies; and power was given unto him to continue forty and two months. 6 <u>And he opened his mouth in blasphemy against God, to blaspheme his name, and his tabernacle, and them that dwell in heaven.</u> 7 And it was given unto him to make war with the saints, and to overcome them: and power was given him over all kindreds, and tongues, and nations.*[85]

Not only did we see the dragon being wroth with the woman and going *"to make war with the remnant of her seed which keep the commandments of God, and have the testimony of Jesus Christ"*, we also see the Antichrist being given power over the entirety of the earth to *"make war with the saints and to overcome them"*. Thus, we know they do not all flee. This point is further underscored in Daniel 11.

> *Daniel 11:36 <u>And the king shall do according to his will; and he shall exalt himself, and magnify himself above every god, and shall speak marvellous things against the God of gods,</u> and shall prosper till the indignation be accomplished: for that that is determined shall be done.*[86]

This same point is illustrated in II Thessalonians 2.

> *II Thessalonians 2:4 Who opposeth and exalteth himself above all that is called God, or that is worshipped; so that he as God sitteth in the temple of God, shewing himself that he is God.*[87]

I think it's fair to say we can infer from these three passages the Abomination of Desolation will be the self-proclamation and self-exaltation of the Antichrist above God and all that is called God, which is to say the entirety of the Trinity. Setting up a statue or sacrificing an unclean animal on the altar is likely not something that will lead to the Antichrist being tossed into the lake of fire 1000 years earlier than everyone else. Proclaiming himself to be above God so that he is worshipped as God… will. It will also send the Jews fleeing, because the same thing that led to their rejection of Jesus (making Himself equal with God) will cause them to reject the Antichrist as their messiah (declaring himself to be <u>above</u> God).

Finally, the reference to the Antichrist prospering "*till the indignation be accomplished*" is a reference to the final 42 months of the Week, during which he will have power over the whole of the earth (except for the supernaturally protected remnant). His power will come to an abrupt halt at the end of the 70th Week, with the return of Jesus Christ.

The End of the 70th Week

The final portion of Part Two will address part "c" of Daniel 9:27. I will post the last part of the verse in just a moment. Before I do so, I wanted to point out several references in the Scriptures I've already used which illustrate the temporariness of the Antichrist's "time".

> *Daniel 11:36 And the king shall do according to his will; and he shall exalt himself, and magnify himself above every god, and shall speak marvellous things against the God of gods, <u>and shall prosper till the indignation be accomplished</u>: for that that is determined shall be done.*

> *II Thessalonians 2:9 And then shall that Wicked be revealed, <u>whom the Lord shall consume with the spirit of his mouth, and shall destroy with the brightness of his coming</u>:*

Indeed, we also see this in Daniel 9:27 part "c":

> *Daniel 9:27 even until the consummation, and that determined shall be poured upon the desolate.*

The word consummation means "completion". It is a reference to the completion of Daniel's 70th Week. The language used here speaks of the judgment held in store for the "desolator". We see such judgment enacted in both Daniel 7 and Revelation 19 at the Second Coming of Jesus Christ, which will correspond to the end of the beast's 42-month reign of terror.

> *Daniel 7:9 I beheld till the thrones were cast down, and the Ancient of days did sit, whose garment was white as snow, and the hair of his head like the pure wool: his throne was like the fiery flame, and his wheels as burning fire. 10 A fiery stream issued and came forth from before him: thousand thousands ministered unto him, and ten thousand times ten*

thousand stood before him: the judgment was set, and the books were opened. 11 I beheld then because of the voice of the great words which the horn spake: I beheld even till the beast was slain, and his body destroyed, and given to the burning flame.[88]

Revelation 19:11 And I saw heaven opened, and behold a white horse; and he that sat upon him was called Faithful and True, and in righteousness he doth judge and make war. 12 His eyes were as a flame of fire, and on his head were many crowns; and he had a name written, that no man knew, but he himself. 13 And he was clothed with a vesture dipped in blood: and his name is called The Word of God. 14 And the armies which were in heaven followed him upon white horses, clothed in fine linen, white and clean. 15 And out of his mouth goeth a sharp sword, that with it he should smite the nations: and he shall rule them with a rod of iron: and he treadeth the winepress of the fierceness and wrath of Almighty God. 16 And he hath on his vesture and on his thigh a name written, KING OF KINGS, AND LORD OF LORDS. 17 And I saw an angel standing in the sun; and he cried with a loud voice, saying to all the fowls that fly in the midst of heaven, Come and gather yourselves together unto the supper of the great God; 18 That ye may eat the flesh of kings, and the flesh of captains, and the flesh of mighty men, and the flesh of horses, and of them that sit on them, and the flesh of all men, both free and bond, both small and great. 19 And I saw the beast, and the kings of the earth, and their armies, gathered together to make war against him that sat on the horse, and against his army. 20 And the beast was taken, and with him the false prophet that wrought miracles before him, with which he deceived them that had received the mark of the beast, and them that worshipped his image. These both were cast alive into a lake of fire burning with brimstone.[89]

We see from Daniel 7:11 and Revelation 19:20 the Antichrist and False Prophet get special treatment. The rest of the unrighteous will go to Hades to await their final judgment at the Great White Throne, which takes place after the Millennial Reign of Christ. At the Great White Throne, the unrighteous will be cast into the lake of fire where they will spend eternity. However, the Antichrist and the False Prophet get to go there immediately after Jesus's Second Coming, 1000 years before everyone else. They will bypass Hades altogether and go straight to the lake of fire.

Thus, part "c" of Daniel 9:27 will be fulfilled, and Daniel's 70th Week will be complete.

A Summary of Daniel 9:27

We have now addressed all the prophecies contained in Daniel 9:27.

> *Daniel 9:27 And he shall confirm the covenant with many for one week: and in the midst of the week he shall cause the sacrifice and the oblation to cease, and for the overspreading of abominations he shall make it desolate, even until the consummation, and that determined shall be poured upon the desolate.*

The Antichrist will strengthen the Old Covenant, or reinstitute the trappings of the Mosaic Law, with the religious leaders in Israel for a period of seven years. At the midpoint of the Week, he will stop the sacrifices and offerings required by the law, thereby breaking it. He will also set himself up in the temple, declaring himself to be above God and all that is called God which will incite a remnant of Jews to flee. During their flight, God will supernaturally protect them. He will continue to do so for the entire second half of the Week, while Satan and the Antichrist are wreaking havoc on the saints. At the end of the 70th Week, Jesus will return and put an end to all unrighteousness, including the physical persons of the Antichrist and the False Prophet.

It is my hope you now have clarity on the different components of Daniel 9:27 and understand what the covenant is. I hope you understand it is not merely a peace treaty.

Final Thoughts

I cannot stress how important it is for people to believe in the Lord Jesus Christ now, so they can enter a New Covenant relationship with Him. Time is short, and the decision must be made without delay.

> *Matthew 26:26 And as they were eating, Jesus took bread, and blessed it, and brake it, and gave it to the disciples, and said, Take, eat; this is my body. 27 And he took the cup, and gave thanks, and gave it to them, saying, Drink ye all of it; 28 <u>For this is my blood of the new testament, which is shed for many for the remission of sins.</u>*[90]

The blood of animals is insufficient to save. Only the blood of Jesus is sufficient. We will be saved only by our faith in Him. The Gospel of Jesus Christ is found in I Corinthians 15:

> *I Corinthians 15:1 Moreover, brethren, I declare unto you the gospel which I preached unto you, which also ye have received, and wherein ye stand; 2 By which also ye are saved, if ye keep in memory what I preached unto you, unless ye have believed in vain. 3 For I delivered unto you first of all that which I also received, <u>how that Christ died for our sins according to the scriptures; 4 And that he was buried, and that he rose again the third day according to the scriptures:</u>*[91]

This next concept is the most important of all to understand:

> *Acts 4:10 Be it known unto you all, and to all the people of Israel, that by the name of Jesus Christ of Nazareth, whom ye crucified, whom God raised from the dead, even by him doth this man stand here before you whole. 11 This is the stone which was set at nought of you builders, which is become the*

head of the corner. 12 Neither is there salvation in any other: for there is none other name under heaven given among men, whereby we must be saved.[92]

John 14:6 Jesus saith unto him, I am the way, the truth, and the life: no man cometh unto the Father, but by me.[93]

PART THREE: The Feasts of the Lord

An Overview of the Feasts of the Lord

Within the Bible prophecy community, there is a great deal of emphasis placed on the feasts of the Lord and how they might relate to the Second Coming of Jesus Christ. There is also a great deal of debate as to whether the feasts are applicable to the church, or if they are intended for Israel alone. For those reasons, I felt it was necessary to understand what these feasts are, what their purpose is, and how they have historically been fulfilled.

The feasts of the Lord are mentioned in Leviticus 23, and most of them have specific dates on which they are to be celebrated. As we will see shortly, there are seven such feasts. By the end of Part Three, it is my hope you will understand the question *"who are the feasts intended for?"* is only a small part of a bigger picture. Let's begin by going through Leviticus 23 to learn what the seven feasts are so we can more fully understand what their purpose is. When we understand their joint purpose, we can understand for whom they are intended.

Leviticus 23 provides explicit detail about when the feasts of the Lord are to be observed, how long they are to be observed for, the types of sacrifices offered during each, and various other components. It is clear from Leviticus 23:1-2 which group of people is intended in the initial giving of the feasts.

> *Leviticus 23:1 And the LORD spake unto Moses, saying, 2 Speak unto the children of Israel, and say unto them, Concerning the feasts of the LORD, which ye shall proclaim to be holy convocations, even these are my feasts.*[94]

The feasts were given to Israel as part of the law. The church was not in view since it would not exist for another 1500 years, give or take. I will expand on that point in a bit. First, we should understand what a "feast" is.

The word "feast" is the Hebrew word "moed"[95], which means "appointed time". The feasts were specific days set aside during various times of the year to "meet with the Lord". We are further told they were to be "holy convocations". The word "holy" means "sacred" or "set apart".[96] The word "convocation" means "assembly."[97] From these words, we glean the following: the feasts were meetings between God and the entire assembly of Israel, set apart from the "normal course of business".

I don't wish to digress from my main point, but there is one point of clarification I need to make.

Leviticus 23:4 These are the feasts of the LORD, even holy convocations, which ye shall proclaim in their seasons.

Verse 4 speaks of these feasts being proclaimed "in their seasons", leading some to believe they cannot be celebrated outside the parameters of what we would understand to be the four seasons. The word "season" is the word "moed". It simply means "appointed time". It does not relate to winter, spring, summer, or fall. What we have termed the "spring feasts" or "fall feasts" comes from an inaccurate interpretation of the word "seasons". Our seasons, which are dependent upon equinoxes and solstices, are not in view in this verse. The meaning here is simply that the feasts are to be celebrated at their "appointed times".

What are these "feasts"? What are the "appointed times"? Let's begin with an overview of each of the feasts of the Lord.

Leviticus 23:5 In the fourteenth day of the first month at even is the LORD's passover.

The first feast of the Lord is Passover.

> *Leviticus 23:6 And on the fifteenth day of the same month is the feast of unleavened bread unto the LORD: seven days ye must eat unleavened bread. 7 In the first day ye shall have an holy convocation: ye shall do no servile work therein. 8 But ye shall offer an offering made by fire unto the LORD seven days: in the seventh day is an holy convocation: ye shall do no servile work therein.*

The second feast of the Lord is Unleavened Bread.

> *Leviticus 23:9 And the LORD spake unto Moses, saying, 10 Speak unto the children of Israel, and say unto them, When ye be come into the land which I give unto you, and shall reap the harvest thereof, then ye shall bring a sheaf of the firstfruits of your harvest unto the priest: 11 And he shall wave the sheaf before the LORD, to be accepted for you: on the morrow after the sabbath the priest shall wave it. 12 And ye shall offer that day when ye wave the sheaf an he lamb without blemish of the first year for a burnt offering unto the LORD. 13 And the meat offering thereof shall be two tenth deals of fine flour mingled with oil, an offering made by fire unto the LORD for a sweet savour: and the drink offering thereof shall be of wine, the fourth part of an hin. 14 And ye shall eat neither bread, nor parched corn, nor green ears, until the selfsame day that ye have brought an offering unto your God: it shall be a statute for ever throughout your generations in all your dwellings.*

The third feast of the Lord is Firstfruits.

> *Leviticus 23:15 And ye shall count unto you from the morrow after the sabbath, from the day that ye brought the sheaf of the wave offering; seven sabbaths shall be complete: 16 Even unto the morrow after the seventh sabbath shall ye number fifty days; and ye shall offer a new meat offering unto the*

> LORD. *17 Ye shall bring out of your habitations two wave loaves of two tenth deals; they shall be of fine flour; they shall be baken with leaven; they are the firstfruits unto the* LORD. *18 And ye shall offer with the bread seven lambs without blemish of the first year, and one young bullock, and two rams: they shall be for a burnt offering unto the* LORD, *with their meat offering, and their drink offerings, even an offering made by fire, of sweet savour unto the* LORD.
> *19 Then ye shall sacrifice one kid of the goats for a sin offering, and two lambs of the first year for a sacrifice of peace offerings. 20 And the priest shall wave them with the bread of the firstfruits for a wave offering before the* LORD, *with the two lambs: they shall be holy to the* LORD *for the priest. 21 And ye shall proclaim on the selfsame day, that it may be an holy convocation unto you: ye shall do no servile work therein: it shall be a statute for ever in all your dwellings throughout your generations. 22 And when ye reap the harvest of your land, thou shalt not make clean riddance of the corners of thy field when thou reapest, neither shalt thou gather any gleaning of thy harvest: thou shalt leave them unto the poor, and to the stranger: I am the* LORD *your God.*

The fourth feast of the Lord is Weeks, or what we refer to as Pentecost.

> *Leviticus 23:23 And the* LORD *spake unto Moses, saying, 24 Speak unto the children of Israel, saying, In the seventh month, in the first day of the month, shall ye have a sabbath, a memorial of blowing of trumpets, an holy convocation. 25 Ye shall do no servile work therein: but ye shall offer an offering made by fire unto the* LORD.

The fifth feast of the Lord is Trumpets.

> *Leviticus 23:27 Also on the tenth day of this seventh month there shall be a day of atonement: it shall be an holy convocation unto you; and ye shall afflict your souls, and offer an offering made by fire unto the LORD. 28 And ye shall do no work in that same day: for it is a day of atonement, to make an atonement for you before the LORD your God. 29 For whatsoever soul it be that shall not be afflicted in that same day, he shall be cut off from among his people. 30 And whatsoever soul it be that doeth any work in that same day, the same soul will I destroy from among his people. 31 Ye shall do no manner of work: it shall be a statute for ever throughout your generations in all your dwellings. 32 It shall be unto you a sabbath of rest, and ye shall afflict your souls: in the ninth day of the month at even, from even unto even, shall ye celebrate your sabbath.*

The sixth feast of the Lord is the Day of Atonement.

> *Leviticus 23:33 And the LORD spake unto Moses, saying, 34 Speak unto the children of Israel, saying, The fifteenth day of this seventh month shall be the feast of tabernacles for seven days unto the LORD. 35 On the first day shall be an holy convocation: ye shall do no servile work therein. 36 Seven days ye shall offer an offering made by fire unto the LORD: on the eighth day shall be an holy convocation unto you; and ye shall offer an offering made by fire unto the LORD: it is a solemn assembly; and ye shall do no servile work therein. 37 These are the feasts of the LORD, which ye shall proclaim to be holy convocations, to offer an offering made by fire unto the LORD, a burnt offering, and a meat offering, a sacrifice, and drink offerings, every thing upon his day: 38 Beside the sabbaths of the LORD, and beside your gifts, and beside all your vows, and beside all your freewill offerings, which ye give unto the LORD. 39 Also in the fifteenth day of the seventh month, when ye have gathered in*

the fruit of the land, ye shall keep a feast unto the LORD seven days: on the first day shall be a sabbath, and on the eighth day shall be a sabbath. 40 And ye shall take you on the first day the boughs of goodly trees, branches of palm trees, and the boughs of thick trees, and willows of the brook; and ye shall rejoice before the LORD your God seven days. 41 And ye shall keep it a feast unto the LORD seven days in the year. It shall be a statute for ever in your generations: ye shall celebrate it in the seventh month. 42 Ye shall dwell in booths seven days; all that are Israelites born shall dwell in booths: 43 That your generations may know that I made the children of Israel to dwell in booths, when I brought them out of the land of Egypt: I am the LORD your God.

The seventh feast of the Lord is Tabernacles.

Leviticus 23:44 And Moses declared unto the children of Israel the feasts of the LORD.

A Shadow of Things to Come

We know from Leviticus 23:2 the feasts of the Lord were given to Israel. Colossians 2 helps us determine who the feasts are intended for today.

> *Colossians 2:16 Let no man therefore judge you in meat, or in drink, or in respect of an holyday, or of the new moon, or of the sabbath days: 17 Which are a shadow of things to come; but the body is of Christ.*[98]

In those two verses in Colossians, we achieve a very fundamental understanding. The feasts, or "holy days", are a shadow of things to come. A shadow is not the substance. Rather, it is a representation or an indication something or someone is coming. In the case of the feasts, we are told they are a shadow, but the body is of Christ. More specifically, the feasts of the Lord point to the coming of Jesus Christ.

> *Matthew 5:17 Think not that I am come to destroy the law, or the prophets: I am not come to destroy, but to fulfil.*[99]

I included Matthew 5:17, because the feasts are part of the Levitical law, given to Israel. Jesus came to fulfill the law, and He did. Since part of the law which He fulfilled includes the feasts, we can safely say the feasts have all found fulfillment in the person of Jesus Christ.

This idea is either not known or not understood among a large majority of the church. Until recently, I was also in that camp. Most prophecy teachers teach that Jesus will fulfill the "fall feasts" at His Second Coming, just as He fulfilled the "spring feasts" at His First Coming. While there is nothing to suggest the feasts cannot or will not have dual fulfillments, all the feasts of the Lord have already found fulfillment in the person of Jesus Christ. This idea might be

radical for some, so let's look and see how this has been the case.
We will start with the first feast mentioned in Leviticus 23: Passover.

The Feast of Passover

The text below may seem familiar if you read Parts One and Two regarding the discussion of the first 69 Weeks.

> *Daniel 9:25 Know therefore and understand, that from the going forth of the commandment to restore and to build Jerusalem unto the Messiah the Prince shall be seven weeks, and threescore and two weeks: the street shall be built again, and the wall, even in troublous times. 26 And after threescore and two weeks shall Messiah be cut off, but not for himself: and the people of the prince that shall come shall destroy the city and the sanctuary; and the end thereof shall be with a flood, and unto the end of the war desolations are determined.*[100]

The first 69 Weeks of years have already been fulfilled. The decree to restore and rebuild Jerusalem was given by Artaxerxes on March 14, 445 B.C. From there, a day count of 173,880 days ends us up at Palm Sunday, April 6, 32 A.D.[101]

7 Weeks x 7 years per Week x 360 days per year = 17,640 days
62 Weeks x 7 years per Week x 360 days per year = 156,240 days

17,640 + 156,240 = 173,880 days in 69 Weeks

It was at the end of that very day count, on Palm Sunday, Jesus rode into Jerusalem on a donkey and presented Himself as the Lamb of God who would be sacrificed on Passover, four days later.

> *Matthew 21:5 Tell ye the daughter of Sion, Behold, thy King cometh unto thee, meek, and sitting upon an ass, and a colt the foal of an ass. 6 And the disciples went, and did as Jesus commanded them, 7 And brought the ass, and the colt, and put on them their clothes, and they set him thereon. 8 And a*

> *very great multitude spread their garments in the way; others cut down branches from the trees, and strawed them in the way. 9 And the multitudes that went before, and that followed, cried, saying, Hosanna to the son of David: Blessed is he that cometh in the name of the Lord; Hosanna in the highest. 10 And when he was come into Jerusalem, all the city was moved, saying, Who is this? 11 And the multitude said, This is Jesus the prophet of Nazareth of Galilee.[102]*

Daniel 9:26 tells us after the conclusion of the first 69 Weeks, Messiah would be "cut off", or killed, but not for Himself. Rather, He laid down His life for us, taking upon Himself the sins of the world. Thus, the New Covenant was established, and the "age of grace", also referred to as the church age, was born.

Jesus Christ was the Passover Lamb. I Corinthians 5:7 tells us as much.

> *I Corinthians 5:7 Purge out therefore the old leaven, that ye may be a new lump, as ye are unleavened. For even Christ our passover is sacrificed for us:[103]*

Indeed, even from the beginning of His ministry, He had been proclaimed as such.

> *John 1:29 The next day John seeth Jesus coming unto him, and saith, Behold the Lamb of God, which taketh away the sin of the world.[104]*

Jesus Christ died on the cross for the sins of the world on Passover. Thus, we have the fulfillment of the Feast of Passover in the person of Jesus Christ.

The Feast of Unleavened Bread

The second feast of the Lord is Unleavened Bread. Unleavened bread is pierced and striped so it will not rise. Leaven also represents sin. Jesus was the sinless Son of God, crucified for the sins of the world. Jesus's atonement for sins which were not His own is the only time in human history where God has allowed an innocent party to pay for the sins of the guilty.

> *Isaiah 53:1 Who hath believed our report? and to whom is the arm of the LORD revealed? 2 For he shall grow up before him as a tender plant, and as a root out of a dry ground: he hath no form nor comeliness; and when we shall see him, there is no beauty that we should desire him. 3 He is despised and rejected of men; a man of sorrows, and acquainted with grief: and we hid as it were our faces from him; he was despised, and we esteemed him not. 4 Surely he hath borne our griefs, and carried our sorrows: yet we did esteem him stricken, smitten of God, and afflicted. 5 But he was wounded for our transgressions, he was bruised for our iniquities: the chastisement of our peace was upon him; and with his stripes we are healed. 6 All we like sheep have gone astray; we have turned every one to his own way; and the LORD hath laid on him the iniquity of us all. 7 He was oppressed, and he was afflicted, yet he opened not his mouth: he is brought as a lamb to the slaughter, and as a sheep before her shearers is dumb, so he openeth not his mouth. 8 He was taken from prison and from judgment: and who shall declare his generation? for he was cut off out of the land of the living: for the transgression of my people was he stricken. 9 And he made his grave with the wicked, and with the rich in his death; because he had done no violence, neither was any deceit in his mouth. 10 Yet it pleased the LORD to bruise him; he hath put him to grief: when thou shalt make his soul an offering for sin, he shall see his seed, he shall prolong his*

days, and the pleasure of the LORD *shall prosper in his hand. 11 He shall see of the travail of his soul, and shall be satisfied: by his knowledge shall my righteous servant justify many; for he shall bear their iniquities.*[105]

After He laid down His life for our sins, Jesus was removed from the cross and buried in a tomb.

Matthew 27:54 Now when the centurion, and they that were with him, watching Jesus, saw the earthquake, and those things that were done, they feared greatly, saying, Truly this was the Son of God. 55 And many women were there beholding afar off, which followed Jesus from Galilee, ministering unto him: 56 Among which was Mary Magdalene, and Mary the mother of James and Joses, and the mother of Zebedees children. 57 When the even was come, there came a rich man of Arimathaea, named Joseph, who also himself was Jesus' disciple: 58 He went to Pilate, and begged the body of Jesus. Then Pilate commanded the body to be delivered. 59 And when Joseph had taken the body, he wrapped it in a clean linen cloth, 60 And laid it in his own new tomb, which he had hewn out in the rock: and he rolled a great stone to the door of the sepulchre, and departed.[106]

It was in this very tomb the body of Jesus laid for three days. What occurred during those three days is also important.

Colossians 2:13 And you, being dead in your sins and the uncircumcision of your flesh, hath he quickened together with him, having forgiven you all trespasses; 14 Blotting out the handwriting of ordinances that was against us, which was contrary to us, and took it out of the way, nailing it to his cross; 15 And having spoiled principalities and powers, he made a shew of them openly, triumphing over them in it.[107]

We also read of this in Ephesians 4.

> *Ephesians 4:8 Wherefore he saith, When he ascended up on high, he led captivity captive, and gave gifts unto men. 9 (Now that he ascended, what is it but that he also descended first into the lower parts of the earth? 10 He that descended is the same also that ascended up far above all heavens, that he might fill all things.)*[108]

During those three days, Jesus descended into the lower parts of the earth to triumph over evil and to preach the Gospel to those in Abraham's Bosom, afterward taking them up to be with the Father. There, the saints await their resurrection.

> *I Corinthians 5:8 Therefore let us keep the feast, not with old leaven, neither with the leaven of malice and wickedness; but with the unleavened bread of sincerity and truth.*

Thus, we have the fulfillment of the Feast of Unleavened Bread in the person of Jesus Christ.

The Feast of Firstfruits

On the third day, Jesus rose from the grave.

> *Matthew 28:1 In the end of the sabbath, as it began to dawn toward the first day of the week, came Mary Magdalene and the other Mary to see the sepulchre. 2 And, behold, there was a great earthquake: for the angel of the Lord descended from heaven, and came and rolled back the stone from the door, and sat upon it. 3 His countenance was like lightning, and his raiment white as snow: 4 And for fear of him the keepers did shake, and became as dead men. 5 And the angel answered and said unto the women, Fear not ye: for I know that ye seek Jesus, which was crucified. 6 He is not here: for he is risen, as he said. Come, see the place where the Lord lay.*[109]

We see Jesus specifically referenced as the firstfruits of them that slept, or of the dead, in I Corinthians 15.

> *I Corinthians 15:19 If in this life only we have hope in Christ, we are of all men most miserable. 20 But now is Christ risen from the dead, and become the firstfruits of them that slept. 21 For since by man came death, by man came also the resurrection of the dead. 22 For as in Adam all die, even so in Christ shall all be made alive.*[110]

It is within the fulfillments of the first three feasts of the Lord we see the Gospel of Jesus Christ brought to life.

> *I Corinthians 15:1 Moreover, brethren, I declare unto you the gospel which I preached unto you, which also ye have received, and wherein ye stand; 2 By which also ye are saved, if ye keep in memory what I preached unto you, unless ye have believed in vain. 3 For I delivered unto you first of all that which I also received, how that Christ died for our*

sins according to the scriptures; 4 And that he was buried, and that he rose again the third day according to the scriptures:[111]

The Gospel of Jesus Christ is the "open door" referenced in Revelation 3:8 wherein Jesus says, *"behold, I have set before thee an open door, and no man can shut it:"*[112] Since its inception, the Gospel message has been preached throughout all nations as part of the Great Commission. It will cease going forth when Jesus Christ returns at the Second Coming and effectively shuts the "open door".

Thus, we have the fulfillment of the Feast of Firstfruits in the person of Jesus Christ.

The Feast of Weeks

The feast of Weeks is more commonly referred to as Pentecost. Pentecost is derived from the Greek word "pentēkostē"[113], meaning "fiftieth". It would be 50 days after Jesus rose from the grave fulfilling Firstfruits wherein the feast of Weeks would find its fulfillment. However, Jesus would no longer be on earth when Pentecost was fulfilled. Knowing He would be leaving, Jesus told His disciples of the gift He would be sending for them in His absence. This gift was to be the Comforter, otherwise known as the Holy Spirit.

> *John 14:16 And I will pray the Father, and he shall give you another Comforter, that he may abide with you for ever; 17 Even the Spirit of truth; whom the world cannot receive, because it seeth him not, neither knoweth him: but ye know him; for he dwelleth with you, and shall be in you. 18 I will not leave you comfortless: I will come to you. 19 Yet a little while, and the world seeth me no more; but ye see me: because I live, ye shall live also. 20 At that day ye shall know that I am in my Father, and ye in me, and I in you.*

> *John 14:25 These things have I spoken unto you, being yet present with you. 26 But the Comforter, which is the Holy Ghost, whom the Father will send in my name, he shall teach you all things, and bring all things to your remembrance, whatsoever I have said unto you. 27 Peace I leave with you, my peace I give unto you: not as the world giveth, give I unto you. Let not your heart be troubled, neither let it be afraid. 28 Ye have heard how I said unto you, I go away, and come again unto you. If ye loved me, ye would rejoice, because I said, I go unto the Father: for my Father is greater than I. 29 And now I have told you before it come to pass, that, when it is come to pass, ye might believe.*[114]

As He was preparing to leave them, Jesus told His disciples to wait in Jerusalem for the arrival of the promised Comforter. Then, He ascended to heaven.

> *Acts 1:4 And, being assembled together with them, commanded them that they should not depart from Jerusalem, but wait for the promise of the Father, which, saith he, ye have heard of me. 5 For John truly baptized with water; but ye shall be baptized with the Holy Ghost not many days hence. 6 When they therefore were come together, they asked of him, saying, Lord, wilt thou at this time restore again the kingdom to Israel? 7 And he said unto them, It is not for you to know the times or the seasons, which the Father hath put in his own power. 8 But ye shall receive power, after that the Holy Ghost is come upon you: and ye shall be witnesses unto me both in Jerusalem, and in all Judaea, and in Samaria, and unto the uttermost part of the earth. 9 And when he had spoken these things, while they beheld, he was taken up; and a cloud received him out of their sight.*[115]

The disciples followed Jesus's instruction to wait in Jerusalem. Ten days after He ascended, they did indeed receive His gift.

> *Acts 2:1 And when the day of Pentecost was fully come, they were all with one accord in one place. 2 And suddenly there came a sound from heaven as of a rushing mighty wind, and it filled all the house where they were sitting. 3 And there appeared unto them cloven tongues like as of fire, and it sat upon each of them. 4 And they were all filled with the Holy Ghost, and began to speak with other tongues, as the Spirit gave them utterance. 5 And there were dwelling at Jerusalem Jews, devout men, out of every nation under heaven. 6 Now when this was noised abroad, the multitude came together, and were confounded, because that every man heard them*

speak in his own language. 7 And they were all amazed and marvelled, saying one to another, Behold, are not all these which speak Galilaeans? 8 And how hear we every man in our own tongue, wherein we were born? 9 Parthians, and Medes, and Elamites, and the dwellers in Mesopotamia, and in Judaea, and Cappadocia, in Pontus, and Asia, 10 Phrygia, and Pamphylia, in Egypt, and in the parts of Libya about Cyrene, and strangers of Rome, Jews and proselytes, 11 Cretes and Arabians, we do hear them speak in our tongues the wonderful works of God.[116]

Thus, we have the fulfillment of the Feast of Weeks, or Pentecost, in the person of Jesus Christ. The Father sent the Spirit in Jesus's name in accordance with the promise Jesus made.

The Waiting Church

It is important to point out Jesus has been in heaven since He ascended. John 14 contains the promise He made to return for us.

> *John 14:1 Let not your heart be troubled: ye believe in God, believe also in me. 2 In my Father's house are many mansions: if it were not so, I would have told you. I go to prepare a place for you. 3 And if I go and prepare a place for you, I will come again, and receive you unto myself; that where I am, there ye may be also. 4 And whither I go ye know, and the way ye know. 5 Thomas saith unto him, Lord, we know not whither thou goest; and how can we know the way? 6 Jesus saith unto him, I am the way, the truth, and the life: no man cometh unto the Father, but by me. 7 If ye had known me, ye should have known my Father also: and from henceforth ye know him, and have seen him.*[117]

The Holy Spirit, given on Pentecost, is the down payment on our inheritance. Receiving the Holy Spirit after believing in Jesus Christ is how we are sealed, or set apart unto God, for the day of our redemption.

> *Ephesians 1:13 In whom ye also trusted, after that ye heard the word of truth, the gospel of your salvation: in whom also after that ye believed, ye were sealed with that holy Spirit of promise, 14 Which is the earnest of our inheritance until the redemption of the purchased possession, unto the praise of his glory.*[118]

> *Romans 8:14 For as many as are led by the Spirit of God, they are the sons of God. 15 For ye have not received the spirit of bondage again to fear; but ye have received the Spirit of adoption, whereby we cry, Abba, Father. 16 The Spirit itself beareth witness with our spirit, that we are the*

> *children of God: 17 And if children, then heirs; heirs of God, and joint-heirs with Christ; if so be that we suffer with him, that we may be also glorified together.*[119]

The day of our redemption is the day Jesus returns for us. It is our "blessed hope", the rapture of the church.

> *Titus 2:13 Looking for that blessed hope, and the glorious appearing of the great God and our Saviour Jesus Christ;*[120]

It must be noted the rapture of the church is not the same as the Second Coming of Christ. Rather, the rapture of the church fulfills the promise Jesus made in Revelation 3:10. It is yet another substantiation for a pre-tribulational rapture of the church.

> *Revelation 3:10 Because thou hast kept the word of my patience, I also will keep thee from the hour of temptation, which shall come upon all the world, to try them that dwell upon the earth.*[121]

After the fulfillment of the first four feasts of the Lord, many people say there has been a break which leaves the remaining three feasts unfulfilled. This could appear to be the case since Jesus has not been on earth since His ascension to continue fulfilling them. Thus, they might say we could speculate about how the final three feasts might find fulfillment at the Second Coming.

There is a lot of research available regarding possible fulfillments for the "fall feasts" which detail types, shadows, and patterns. However, I'm going to take a different tack and show you how we don't necessarily need all those speculations, types, shadows, and patterns. The fulfillments of the other three feasts have already been accomplished. That does not mean there couldn't be dual fulfillments. It only means it is not necessary for there to be.

Let's begin by looking at the fulfillment of the fifth feast of the Lord: Trumpets.

The Feast of Trumpets

It was regarding the fulfillment of the Feast of Trumpets where I had an "a-ha moment". This was the last one to fall into place for me, and I basically had to throw all the research I had done out the window. While my previous research may or may not be valid, understanding the feasts have already been fulfilled utterly changed the way I view the end times. When you no longer believe things <u>must</u> happen a certain way, you stop forcing them to fit and start letting the Scripture interpret itself. Hopefully, you will see what I mean. Let's start by looking at what Leviticus 23 says about the Feast of Trumpets.

> *Leviticus 23:23 And the LORD spake unto Moses, saying, 24 Speak unto the children of Israel, saying, In the seventh month, in the first day of the month, shall ye have a sabbath, a memorial of blowing of trumpets, an holy convocation. 25 Ye shall do no servile work therein: but ye shall offer an offering made by fire unto the LORD.*

Those verses tell us a few different things. First, we see this feast was to be celebrated on the first day of the seventh month, or on Tishri 1. The month of Tishri is the start of the Hebrew civil year, as opposed to the start of the religious year which occurs in the month of Nisan, or Abib. We further see Tishri 1 was to be a sabbath day, or a day of rest. It was to be a "holy convocation", which if you recall from previous discussion, means a "set apart assembly". An offering was to be made to the Lord. Finally, they were to celebrate the day as a *"memorial of blowing of trumpets"*.

A Memorial of Blowing of Trumpets

The word "memorial" is the Hebrew word "zikkaron",[122] meaning "remembrance". The following is an excerpt from www.jewsforjesus.org:

> *"The only other reference to this festival in the Torah (Pentateuch) is Numbers 29:1ff. Neither passage provides much information regarding the original meaning of this feast. But, by examining the text in Leviticus 23, we note that the day was to be a memorial with blowing of trumpets. This is our only clue. The word "memorial" indicates that the event to be remembered had taken place prior to this ordinance.*
>
> *To solve the puzzle, we must ask ourselves what extremely significant event, involving the blowing of trumpets, took place in the national life of Israel? What spiritual event was of such great importance that God commanded the people to remember it every year? I believe the Bible points to one outstanding event—connected to the blowing of trumpets—that required memorializing."*[123]

Indeed, there was only one event of such significance. We find it written about in Exodus 19.

> *Exodus 19:5 Now therefore, if ye will obey my voice indeed, and keep my covenant, then ye shall be a peculiar treasure unto me above all people: for all the earth is mine: 6 And ye shall be unto me a kingdom of priests, and an holy nation. These are the words which thou shalt speak unto the children of Israel. 7 And Moses came and called for the elders of the people, and laid before their faces all these words which the LORD commanded him. 8 And all the people answered together, and said, All that the LORD hath spoken we will do.*

And Moses returned the words of the people unto the LORD. 9 And the LORD said unto Moses, Lo, I come unto thee in a thick cloud, that the people may hear when I speak with thee, and believe thee for ever. And Moses told the words of the people unto the LORD.

16 And it came to pass on the third day in the morning, that there were thunders and lightnings, and a thick cloud upon the mount, and the voice of the trumpet exceeding loud; so that all the people that was in the camp trembled. 17 And Moses brought forth the people out of the camp to meet with God; and they stood at the nether part of the mount. 18 And mount Sinai was altogether on a smoke, because the LORD descended upon it in fire: and the smoke thereof ascended as the smoke of a furnace, and the whole mount quaked greatly. 19 And when the voice of the trumpet sounded long, and waxed louder and louder, Moses spake, and God answered him by a voice. 20 And the LORD came down upon mount Sinai, on the top of the mount: and the LORD called Moses up to the top of the mount; and Moses went up.[124]

This is the event for which the feast of Trumpets is a memorial – the giving of the law on Sinai.

"In Exodus chapters 19 and 20 we read the account of God's appearance on Mount Sinai and the initial giving of the Ten Commandments. Exodus 19:5 depicts God inviting the children of Israel into a covenant: the Mosaic Covenant. In a spectacular revelation, God manifested His presence in the smoke and fire on Mount Sinai—as He came to covenant with His people amidst the sound of a trumpet that caused the people to tremble. They promised to do everything that the Lord commanded."[125]

I understand this might be the toughest pill to swallow of all the feast fulfillments, if for no other reason than the giving of the law did not occur on the feast of Trumpets. All the other feasts were fulfilled on their respective feast dates. To put any prospective uneasiness to rest about this, simply type the search term "trumpet" into an online Bible. I use www.biblegateway.com. You will quickly see the only occurrences of the word "trumpet" prior to being used in Leviticus 23 are in Exodus. They relate solely to the giving of the law on Sinai.[126] There is literally nothing else related to trumpets which the Feast of Trumpets could memorialize.

The Final Lawgiver

When God spoke on Sinai, the entire Israelite camp assembled at the base of the mount to listen. The fulfillment of the Feast of Trumpets as it regards the person of Jesus Christ is just as simple: He was the final lawgiver, and they all gathered to Him to listen.

> *Genesis 49:10 The sceptre shall not depart from Judah, nor a lawgiver from between his feet, until Shiloh come; and unto him shall the gathering of the people be.*[127]

Isaiah 33 says something similar.

> *Isaiah 33:22 For the LORD is our judge, the LORD is our lawgiver, the LORD is our king; he will save us.*

Here is an excerpt about this topic from www.1888mpm.org:

> *Indeed, the fact that Christ is a part of the Godhead, possessing all the attributes of Divinity, being the equal of the Father in all respects, as Creator and Lawgiver, is the only force there is in the atonement. It is this, alone which makes redemption a possibility. Christ died "that he might bring us to God" (1 Peter 3:18), but if He lacked one iota of being equal to God, He could not bring us to Him. Divinity means having the attributes of Deity. If Christ were not Divine, then we should have only a human sacrifice. It matters not, even if it were granted that Christ was the highest created intelligence in the universe; in that case He would be a subject, owing allegiance to the law, without ability to do any more than His own duty. He could have no righteousness to impart to others. There is an infinite distance between the highest angel ever created and God; therefore, the highest angel could not lift fallen man up and make him partaker of the Divine nature. Angels can*

> *minister; God only can redeem. Thanks be to God that we are saved "through the redemption that is in Christ Jesus," in whom dwells all the fullness of the Godhead bodily and who is, therefore, able to save to the uttermost them that come unto God by Him.*
>
> <u>*This truth helps to a more perfect understanding of the reason why Christ is called the Word of God. He is the One through whom the Divine will and the Divine power are made known to men. He is, so to speak, the mouthpiece of Divinity, the manifestation of the Godhead. He declares or makes God known to man.*</u> *It pleased the Father that in Him should all fullness dwell; and therefore the Father is not relegated to a secondary position, as some imagine, when* <u>*Christ is exalted as Creator and Lawgiver*</u>*, for the glory of the Father shines through the Son. Since God is known only through Christ, it is evident that the Father cannot be honored, as He ought to be honored, by those who do not exalt Christ. As Christ Himself said, "He that honoreth not the Son honoreth not the Father which hath sent Him." John 5:23*[128]

Thus, we have the fulfillment of the Feast of Trumpets in the person of Jesus Christ.

It is also important to mention there will be another time when the voice of God, as it were of a trumpet, will be used to call an assembly – at the rapture of the church.

> *I Thessalonians 4:16 For the Lord himself shall descend from heaven with a shout, with the voice of the archangel, and with the trump of God: and the dead in Christ shall rise first: 17 Then we which are alive and remain shall be caught up together with them in the clouds, to meet the Lord in the air: and so shall we ever be with the Lord.*[129]

Revelation 4:1 After this I looked, and, behold, a door was opened in heaven: and the first voice which I heard was as it were of a trumpet talking with me; which said, Come up hither, and I will shew thee things which must be hereafter.[130]

The Day of Atonement

This is a relatively new find for me, but I think it is quite interesting. I touched on this when researching why Jesus was baptized. It was then I found out His baptism more than likely occurred on the Day of Atonement. First, it is important to understand why Jesus was baptized. The following is an explanation provided by Dr. J. Vernon McGee:

Q & A: Why Was Jesus Baptized When He Had No Sin?

> *A: Jesus was baptized because He was taking our place. This reveals His perfect identification with us; He took the place of the sinners. When He came to John the Baptist, John did not want to baptize Him at all. Far be it from John, he wasn't going to do it! But the Lord Jesus said, "...It becometh us to fulfil all righteousness" (Matthew 3:15). How is that? Well, He's taking the place of a sinner, and that is realized in His death. When He died upon the cross, He died as a sinner. Now at the very beginning He takes that place of perfect humanity down here, the place actually of a sinner. He was made "sin for us, who knew no sin" (2 Corinthians 5:21). I think the explanation is found in that. He's perfectly identifying Himself with the human family in the baptism.*[131]

Jesus's baptism is found in Matthew 3. We will need to go through parts of Matthew 3 and 4 and look at the events which occurred on that day, what happened directly afterward, and how said events link to the Day of Atonement. Before we get there, though, let's look at what Leviticus 23 says about this sixth feast of the Lord.

> *Leviticus 23:27 Also on the tenth day of this seventh month there shall be a day of atonement: it shall be an holy convocation unto you; and ye shall afflict your souls, and offer an offering made by fire unto the LORD. 28 And ye shall*

> *do no work in that same day: for it is a day of atonement, to make an atonement for you before the LORD your God. 29 For whatsoever soul it be that shall not be afflicted in that same day, he shall be cut off from among his people. 30 And whatsoever soul it be that doeth any work in that same day, the same soul will I destroy from among his people. 31 Ye shall do no manner of work: it shall be a statute for ever throughout your generations in all your dwellings. 32 It shall be unto you a sabbath of rest, and ye shall afflict your souls: in the ninth day of the month at even, from even unto even, shall ye celebrate your sabbath.*

The Day of Atonement occurs on Tishri 10. This feast is a bit different from the others in that it is to be a complete sabbath. Israel is to do no work, and she uses this time to repent to her God. Leviticus 16 gives us additional insight into the Day of Atonement. Let's look at some key verses in the chapter.

> *Leviticus 16:2 And the LORD said unto Moses, Speak unto Aaron thy brother, that he come not at all times into the holy place within the vail before the mercy seat, which is upon the ark; that he die not: for I will appear in the cloud upon the mercy seat. 3 Thus shall Aaron come into the holy place: with a young bullock for a sin offering, and a ram for a burnt offering. 4 He shall put on the holy linen coat, and he shall have the linen breeches upon his flesh, and shall be girded with a linen girdle, and with the linen mitre shall he be attired: these are holy garments; therefore shall he wash his flesh in water, and so put them on. 5 And he shall take of the congregation of the children of Israel two kids of the goats for a sin offering, and one ram for a burnt offering. 6 And Aaron shall offer his bullock of the sin offering, which is for himself, and make an atonement for himself, and for his house. 7 And he shall take the two goats, and present them before the LORD at the door of the tabernacle of the*

> *congregation. 8 And Aaron shall cast lots upon the two goats; one lot for the LORD, and the other lot for the scapegoat. 9 And Aaron shall bring the goat upon which the LORD's lot fell, and offer him for a sin offering. 10 But the goat, on which the lot fell to be the scapegoat, shall be presented alive before the LORD, to make an atonement with him, and to let him go for a scapegoat into the wilderness.* [132]

The high priest was the only person ever allowed to enter the Holy of Holies. He was only allowed to do so once a year, on the Day of Atonement. On this day, the Lord would descend in a cloud to cover the mercy seat. The high priest would then proceed to make atonement, first for himself and his family, then for the sins of national Israel.

> *Leviticus 16:11 And Aaron shall bring the bullock of the sin offering, which is for himself, and shall make an atonement for himself, and for his house, and shall kill the bullock of the sin offering which is for himself: 12 And he shall take a censer full of burning coals of fire from off the altar before the LORD, and his hands full of sweet incense beaten small, and bring it within the vail: 13 And he shall put the incense upon the fire before the LORD, that the cloud of the incense may cover the mercy seat that is upon the testimony, that he die not: 14 And he shall take of the blood of the bullock, and sprinkle it with his finger upon the mercy seat eastward; and before the mercy seat shall he sprinkle of the blood with his finger seven times. 15 Then shall he kill the goat of the sin offering, that is for the people, and bring his blood within the vail, and do with that blood as he did with the blood of the bullock, and sprinkle it upon the mercy seat, and before the mercy seat: 16 And he shall make an atonement for the holy place, because of the uncleanness of the children of Israel, and because of their transgressions in all their sins: and so shall he do for the tabernacle of the congregation, that*

*remaineth among them in the midst of their uncleanness.
17 And there shall be no man in the tabernacle of the congregation when he goeth in to make an atonement in the holy place, until he come out, and have made an atonement for himself, and for his household, and for all the congregation of Israel. 18 And he shall go out unto the altar that is before the LORD, and make an atonement for it; and shall take of the blood of the bullock, and of the blood of the goat, and put it upon the horns of the altar round about. 19 And he shall sprinkle of the blood upon it with his finger seven times, and cleanse it, and hallow it from the uncleanness of the children of Israel. 20 And when he hath made an end of reconciling the holy place, and the tabernacle of the congregation, and the altar, he shall bring the live goat: 21 And Aaron shall lay both his hands upon the head of the live goat, and confess over him all the iniquities of the children of Israel, and all their transgressions in all their sins, putting them upon the head of the goat, and shall send him away by the hand of a fit man into the wilderness: 22 And the goat shall bear upon him all their iniquities unto a land not inhabited: and he shall let go the goat in the wilderness.*

For himself and his family, the high priest selected a bull for a sin offering. Two goats would then be selected for the sins of national Israel. This is precisely what the baptism of Jesus did; it selected Jesus as the offering for sin which would later be performed on the cross. And just as God would descend in a cloud to cover the mercy seat on the Day of Atonement, at Jesus's baptism the Spirit of God descended upon Him like a dove.

Matthew 3:13 Then cometh Jesus from Galilee to Jordan unto John, to be baptized of him. 14 But John forbad him, saying, I have need to be baptized of thee, and comest thou to me? 15 And Jesus answering said unto him, Suffer it to be so

> *now: for thus it becometh us to fulfil all righteousness. Then he suffered him. 16 And Jesus, when he was baptized, went up straightway out of the water: and, lo, the heavens were opened unto him, and he saw the Spirit of God descending like a dove, and lighting upon him: 17 And lo a voice from heaven, saying, This is my beloved Son, in whom I am well pleased.*[133]

As I mentioned, two goat kids would be selected for the sins of national Israel. The high priest would cast lots for the goats, selecting one for the Lord and the other as the scapegoat. On the head of the scapegoat, all the sins of Israel would be laid. The scapegoat was symbolic of the sacrifice Jesus would offer on the cross. Just as the sins of national Israel were laid on the head of the scapegoat, so too were the sins of the world laid upon Jesus's head. It was just as John the Baptist proclaimed on the day of Jesus's baptism – *Behold the Lamb of God, which taketh away the sins of the world.*

> *John 1:26 John answered them, saying, I baptize with water: but there standeth one among you, whom ye know not; 27 He it is, who coming after me is preferred before me, whose shoe's latchet I am not worthy to unloose. 28 These things were done in Bethabara beyond Jordan, where John was baptizing. 29 The next day John seeth Jesus coming unto him, and saith, Behold the Lamb of God, which taketh away the sin of the world. 30 This is he of whom I said, After me cometh a man which is preferred before me: for he was before me. 31 And I knew him not: but that he should be made manifest to Israel, therefore am I come baptizing with water. 32 And John bare record, saying, I saw the Spirit descending from heaven like a dove, and it abode upon him.*[134]

The scapegoat was then sent away from the camp and out into the wilderness. Similarly, Jesus just having been baptized and selected as said scapegoat, also went immediately into the wilderness.

> *Matthew 4:1 Then was Jesus led up of the Spirit into the wilderness to be tempted of the devil.*[135]

We know from many passages in the New Testament, Jesus is our High Priest. He is the mediator of the New Covenant between God and man.

> *1 Timothy 2:5 For there is one God, and one mediator between God and men, the man Christ Jesus;*[136]

> *Hebrews 2:17 Wherefore in all things it behoved him to be made like unto his brethren, that he might be a merciful and faithful high priest in things pertaining to God, to make reconciliation for the sins of the people. 18 For in that he himself hath suffered being tempted, he is able to succour them that are tempted.*[137]

The book of Hebrews strikingly contrasts the sacrifice Christ made on the cross for the New Covenant with the atonement offered under the Old Covenant. The Israelites had to offer atonement annually. Jesus atoned once and for all.

> *Hebrews 9:19 For when Moses had spoken every precept to all the people according to the law, he took the blood of calves and of goats, with water, and scarlet wool, and hyssop, and sprinkled both the book, and all the people, 20 Saying, This is the blood of the testament which God hath enjoined unto you. 21 Moreover he sprinkled with blood both the tabernacle, and all the vessels of the ministry. 22 And almost all things are by the law purged with blood; and without shedding of blood is no remission. 23 It was*

therefore necessary that the patterns of things in the heavens should be purified with these; but the heavenly things themselves with better sacrifices than these. 24 For Christ is not entered into the holy places made with hands, which are the figures of the true; but into heaven itself, now to appear in the presence of God for us: 25 Nor yet that he should offer himself often, as the high priest entereth into the holy place every year with blood of others; 26 For then must he often have suffered since the foundation of the world: but now once in the end of the world hath he appeared to put away sin by the sacrifice of himself.[138]

While the atonement for the sins of the world might not have been complete until He laid down His life on Passover, Jesus was selected as the scapegoat on the Day of Atonement, pronounced by John the Baptist as the One who would take away the sins of the world. Thus, the baptism of Jesus wherein He assumed the place of sinners, beginning the ministry which would end with Him being our scapegoat is how the Day of Atonement found its fulfillment in the person of Jesus Christ.

The Feast of Tabernacles

The feast of Tabernacles is the last of the seven feasts of the Lord. Before we look at its fulfillment, let's go back to Leviticus 23 to see what we are told about it.

> *Leviticus 23:33 And the LORD spake unto Moses, saying, 34 Speak unto the children of Israel, saying, The fifteenth day of this seventh month shall be the feast of tabernacles for seven days unto the LORD. 35 On the first day shall be an holy convocation: ye shall do no servile work therein. 36 Seven days ye shall offer an offering made by fire unto the LORD: on the eighth day shall be an holy convocation unto you; and ye shall offer an offering made by fire unto the LORD: it is a solemn assembly; and ye shall do no servile work therein. 37 These are the feasts of the LORD, which ye shall proclaim to be holy convocations, to offer an offering made by fire unto the LORD, a burnt offering, and a meat offering, a sacrifice, and drink offerings, every thing upon his day: 38 Beside the sabbaths of the LORD, and beside your gifts, and beside all your vows, and beside all your freewill offerings, which ye give unto the LORD. 39 Also in the fifteenth day of the seventh month, when ye have gathered in the fruit of the land, ye shall keep a feast unto the LORD seven days: on the first day shall be a sabbath, and on the eighth day shall be a sabbath. 40 And ye shall take you on the first day the boughs of goodly trees, branches of palm trees, and the boughs of thick trees, and willows of the brook; and ye shall rejoice before the LORD your God seven days. 41 And ye shall keep it a feast unto the LORD seven days in the year. It shall be a statute for ever in your generations: ye shall celebrate it in the seventh month. 42 Ye shall dwell in booths seven days; all that are Israelites born shall dwell in booths: 43 That your generations may know that I made the children*

> *of Israel to dwell in booths, when I brought them out of the land of Egypt: I am the LORD your God.*

The feast of Tabernacles has several components. First, it is a seven-day feast which begins on Tishri 15. The eighth day is a separate feast day called Shemini Atzeret. Both the first day of Tabernacles and Shemini Atzeret are to be sabbath days. Each of the seven days of Tabernacles are characterized by the offering of sacrifices which are to be separate from the normal daily sacrifices. However, there are other details about this feast which make it notable from the others.

Tabernacles is characterized by the waving of palm branches. In ancient times, the waving of palms was a sign of victory. There are only two times in the New Testament the waving of palm branches occurs: in Matthew 21 on Palm Sunday, when Israel was attempting to welcome Jesus as the son of David, or the "Victorious King", and in Revelation 7 where the church is seen in heaven paying homage to their "Victorious King" and Redeemer. It is also interesting to note, and perhaps a bit ironic, Jesus was beaten with the "palms" of hands while being put on trial just prior to His crucifixion. Even in this context, palms were present when Jesus was in the process of gaining "victory" over sin and death.

Tabernacles is also celebrated by dwelling in booths, or temporary dwellings. The Hebrew word for "booth" is "sukkah"; hence, Tabernacles is also called Sukkot. The purpose of dwelling in these booths is to commemorate the 40 years in which Israel wandered in the desert, a temporary dwelling between her exodus from Egypt and her entry into her Promised Land.[139]

Finally, Tabernacles was one of three "pilgrimage" feasts. All male Israelites were required to make their way to Jerusalem annually to attend this feast. It was to be a celebration of the final harvest of the year, which is also why Tabernacles is called the "Feast of Ingathering".

The Word Became Flesh

In the New Testament, the word meaning "to tabernacle, or to dwell as in a tent" is the Greek word "skénoó".[140] It appears only five times. We find the first in John 1.

> *John 1:14 And the Word was made flesh, and dwelt among us, (and we beheld his glory, the glory as of the only begotten of the Father,) full of grace and truth.*[141]

John 1:14 is a reference to the birth of Jesus Christ. Jesus did not come as the fully-grown man who would die for the sins of the world. He came as a baby. God sent Jesus to dwell, or to "tabernacle" among us. Yes, Jesus was born during the feast of Tabernacles. We see further evidence of this in Luke's account of Jesus's birth.

> *Luke 2:7 And she brought forth her firstborn son, and wrapped him in swaddling clothes, and laid him in a manger; because there was no room for them in the inn. 8 And there were in the same country shepherds abiding in the field, keeping watch over their flock by night. 9 And, lo, the angel of the Lord came upon them, and the glory of the Lord shone round about them: and they were sore afraid. 10 And the angel said unto them, Fear not: for, behold, I bring you good tidings of great joy, which shall be to all people. 11 For unto you is born this day in the city of David a Saviour, which is Christ the Lord. 12 And this shall be a sign unto you; Ye shall find the babe wrapped in swaddling clothes, lying in a manger.*[142]

Mary and Joseph could find no room at the inn because of their proximity to Jerusalem during the pilgrimage festival. The cities were packed due to the number of travelers journeying to Jerusalem to participate in the feast of Tabernacles. Thus, they had to seek shelter in a temporary dwelling, a stable for animals. Then, Jesus was laid in a manger. It's very humbling to consider the One whose birth should have been surrounded by the greatest amount of pomp and circumstance ever was born among animals and laid in a manger, which was no more than a feeding trough.

> *Luke 2:13 And suddenly there was with the angel a multitude of the heavenly host praising God, and saying, 14 Glory to God in the highest, and on earth peace, good will toward men.*

The Prince of Peace had been born, sent by the Father to tabernacle amongst those He had been sent to redeem. Thus, we have the fulfillment of the Feast of Tabernacles in the person of Jesus Christ.

Final Thoughts

I hope you now have a better understanding of how all the feasts of the Lord have already found fulfillment in the person of Jesus Christ. I removed many pages of speculative study, because I didn't want to mix conjecture with fact. I decided it was best to keep everything as simple as possible. It all comes down to what Colossians 2 expresses so beautifully:

> *Colossians 2:16 Let no man therefore judge you in meat, or in drink, or in respect of an holyday, or of the new moon, or of the sabbath days: 17 Which are a shadow of things to come; but the body is of Christ.*

The feasts of the Lord were always designed to point to the person of Jesus Christ. The church has never needed to celebrate the feasts, not because they are part of a law which was only given to Israel, nor because Jesus fulfilled that law. Rather, it is because we do not look to things which "represent" Christ. Rather, we look to Christ, Himself.

PART FOUR: The Day of the Lord

The Purposes of the 70 Weeks of Daniel

Hopefully after you finished reading Part Three – The Feasts of the Lord – you aren't left scratching your head and wondering why I included that information in this end times study if those feasts aren't relevant. I'm not suggesting they aren't relevant, only that we need to take a closer look at what we are told about the Second Coming of Jesus Christ to figure out if they do indeed factor in, or if we have been relying too heavily on assumptions. That is what we will begin doing in this part of the study. Let's begin by understanding what the Second Coming of Jesus Christ accomplishes.

Basic information about the events of the Second Coming can be gleaned from Revelation 19, where Jesus is seen leaving heaven with the heavenly armies and returning to earth to put an end to the wickedness which will be running rampant at that time.

> *Revelation 19:11 And I saw heaven opened, and behold a white horse; and he that sat upon him was called Faithful and True, and in righteousness he doth judge and make war. 12 His eyes were as a flame of fire, and on his head were many crowns; and he had a name written, that no man knew, but he himself. 13 And he was clothed with a vesture dipped in blood: and his name is called The Word of God. 14 And the armies which were in heaven followed him upon white horses, clothed in fine linen, white and clean. 15 And out of his mouth goeth a sharp sword, that with it he should smite the nations: and he shall rule them with a rod of iron: and he treadeth the winepress of the fierceness and wrath of Almighty God. 16 And he hath on his vesture and on his thigh a name written, KING OF KINGS, AND LORD OF LORDS. 17 And I saw an angel standing in the sun; and he cried with a loud voice, saying to all the fowls that fly in the midst of heaven, Come and gather yourselves together unto the supper of the*

> *great God; 18 That ye may eat the flesh of kings, and the flesh of captains, and the flesh of mighty men, and the flesh of horses, and of them that sit on them, and the flesh of all men, both free and bond, both small and great. 19 And I saw the beast, and the kings of the earth, and their armies, gathered together to make war against him that sat on the horse, and against his army. 20 And the beast was taken, and with him the false prophet that wrought miracles before him, with which he deceived them that had received the mark of the beast, and them that worshipped his image. These both were cast alive into a lake of fire burning with brimstone. 21 And the remnant were slain with the sword of him that sat upon the horse, which sword proceeded out of his mouth: and all the fowls were filled with their flesh.[143]*

That He will return to judge and make war is only one component of the Second Coming. There are two things Jesus will do when He returns, the first of which is to judge wickedness. Said judgment will take place so the second purpose can be accomplished, which is to bring His Kingdom from heaven to earth. Since His Kingdom will be righteous, all earthly wickedness must be removed. We see both the judgment and Kingdom aspects in play within the purposes for the 70 Weeks of Daniel.

> *Daniel 9:24 Seventy weeks are determined upon thy people and upon thy holy city, to finish the transgression, and to make an end of sins, and to make reconciliation for iniquity, and to bring in everlasting righteousness, and to seal up the vision and prophecy, and to anoint the most Holy.[144]*

There are six purposes the 70 Weeks are designed to accomplish: to finish the transgression, to make an end of sins, to make reconciliation for iniquity, to bring in everlasting righteousness, to seal up the vision and prophecy, and to anoint the most holy. Dr. Arnold Fruchtenbaum wrote about these six purposes and how they may be accomplished.

> *Daniel was next told by Gabriel that the 70 sevens are to accomplish six purposes. The first is **to finish transgression.** The Hebrew word translated "to finish" means "to restrain firmly," "to restrain completely" or "to bring to completion." The Hebrew word translated "transgression" is a very strong word for sin and more literally means "to rebel." The Hebrew text has this word with the definite article, so literally it means "the transgression," or "the rebellion." The point is that some specific act of rebellion is finally going to be completely restrained and brought to an end. This act of rebellion or transgression is to come under complete control so that it will no longer flourish. Israel's apostasy is now to be firmly restrained, in keeping with a similar prediction in Isaiah 59:20.*
>
> *The second purpose of the 70 sevens is **to make an end of sins.** The Hebrew word translated "to make an end" literally means "to seal up" or "to shut up in prison." It means to be securely kept, locked up, not allowed to roam at random. The Hebrew word translated as "sins" literally means "to miss the mark." It refers to sins of daily life, rather than to one specific sin. Even these sins are to be put to an end and taken away. This, too, is quite in keeping with predictions by the prophets that proclaim that in the messianic kingdom, sinning would cease from Israel (Isaiah 27:9, Ezekiel 36:25-27, 37:23, Jeremiah 31:31-34).*
>
> *The third purpose is **to make reconciliation for iniquity**.*

The Hebrew word translated "to make reconciliation" is "kaphar," which has the same root meaning as the word "kippur," as in Yom Kippur. The word "kaphar" literally means "to make atonement." The third purpose, then, is to make atonement in some way for iniquity. In fact, it is by means of this atonement that the first two purposes will also be accomplished, that of finishing the transgression and making an end of sins. The word translated "iniquity" refers to inward sin. This has sometimes been referred to as the sin nature, or perhaps a more common term among Jewish people would be yetzer hara," the evil inclination."

The fourth purpose of the 70 sevens is **to bring in everlasting righteousness.** *More literally this could be translated "to bring in an age of righteousness," since the Hebrew "olam" is better translated as "age" rather than as "everlasting." This age of righteousness is to be the messianic kingdom spoken of in the Prophets (Isaiah 1:26, 11:2-5, 32:17; Jeremiah 23:5-6, 33:15-18). It is this very age that Daniel had been expecting to see established after the 70 years of captivity, but now he is told that will only be after the 490-year period.*

The fifth purpose is **to seal up vision and prophecy.** *Here Daniel used a word which means "to shut up." So "to seal up" means to cause a cessation or to completely fulfill. Thus, vision and prophecy are to be completely fulfilled." Vision" is a reference to oral prophecy, while "prophecy" refers to written prophecy. Both oral and written prophecy will cease with the final fulfillment of all revelations.*

The final purpose of the 70 sevens is **to anoint the most holy.** *A better translation here would be "to anoint a most holy place." This is a reference to the Jewish temple which is to be rebuilt when Messiah comes. It refers to the same*

> *temple that Daniel's contemporary, Ezekiel, described in great detail (Ezekiel 40-48)."*[145]

It is very easy to draw the conclusion the day of judgment will be on Yom Kippur, especially considering what Dr. Fruchtenbaum wrote about the third purpose which is "to make reconciliation for iniquity". It is also easy to draw conclusions about the events of the Second Coming being spread out over several days to fulfill the feasts of Trumpets, Atonement, and Tabernacles, or some combination thereof. Are multiple days in view to accomplish these purposes? Are multiple days required for Jesus to judge then "set up" His Kingdom? I do not believe so.

At His Appearing and His Kingdom

One of the primary verses which got me interested in researching the idea the events of the Second Coming, namely judging the nations and establishing His Kingdom, will all occur on one day was the following verse from II Timothy 4:

> *II Timothy 4:1 I charge thee therefore before God, and the Lord Jesus Christ, who shall judge the quick and the dead at his appearing and his kingdom;[146]*

The ideas presented in this verse tell us when Christ appears in glory, He will exercise all authority given Him as King to judge and to bring His Kingdom to earth. While there is a sequence of events which will manifest on the Day of the Lord beginning with judgment, it is immediately after said judgment those left of the nations, along with the remnant of Israel which the Lord will have delivered, will immediately enter His Kingdom. There are not multiple days involved in that process. It is an either/or scenario with only two options. We see this point illustrated in Matthew 25 with the judgment of the sheep and goats. One will either be condemned, or one will enter His Kingdom. Let's explore this idea a bit further.

> *Matthew 25:31 When the Son of man shall come in his glory, and all the holy angels with him, then shall he sit upon the throne of his glory: 32 And before him shall be gathered all nations: and he shall separate them one from another, as a shepherd divideth his sheep from the goats: 33 And he shall set the sheep on his right hand, but the goats on the left. 34 Then shall the King say unto them on his right hand, Come, ye blessed of my Father, inherit the kingdom prepared for you from the foundation of the world: 35 For I was an hungred, and ye gave me meat: I was thirsty, and ye gave me drink: I was a stranger, and ye took me in: 36 Naked, and ye clothed me: I was sick, and ye visited me: I was in prison,*

and ye came unto me. 37 Then shall the righteous answer him, saying, Lord, when saw we thee an hungred, and fed thee? or thirsty, and gave thee drink? 38 When saw we thee a stranger, and took thee in? or naked, and clothed thee? 39 Or when saw we thee sick, or in prison, and came unto thee? 40 And the King shall answer and say unto them, Verily I say unto you, Inasmuch as ye have done it unto one of the least of these my brethren, ye have done it unto me. 41 Then shall he say also unto them on the left hand, Depart from me, ye cursed, into everlasting fire, prepared for the devil and his angels: 42 For I was an hungred, and ye gave me no meat: I was thirsty, and ye gave me no drink: 43 I was a stranger, and ye took me not in: naked, and ye clothed me not: sick, and in prison, and ye visited me not. 44 Then shall they also answer him, saying, Lord, when saw we thee an hungred, or athirst, or a stranger, or naked, or sick, or in prison, and did not minister unto thee? 45 Then shall he answer them, saying, Verily I say unto you, Inasmuch as ye did it not to one of the least of these, ye did it not to me. 46 And these shall go away into everlasting punishment: but the righteous into life eternal.[147]

It is important to understand this judgment is not for Israel. In Matthew 25:32, we read those gathered before Him will be from "all nations". This is a reference to the Gentile nations. The people of those Gentile nations will then be separated into two groups depending on how they treated His brethren, Israel. Those who helped His brethren will be counted as sheep and granted entry into His Kingdom. Those who did not help His brethren will be counted as goats and told to depart from Him into everlasting punishment. We can read more detailed accounts of how this judgment will occur in Joel 3, Zechariah 12, and Zechariah 14. We will begin with Joel 3, which some may know as the judgment in the Valley of Jehoshaphat, otherwise known as the "valley of decision".

> *Joel 3:1 For, behold, in those days, and in that time, when I shall bring again the captivity of Judah and Jerusalem, 2 I will also gather all nations, and will bring them down into the valley of Jehoshaphat, and will plead with them there for my people and for my heritage Israel, whom they have scattered among the nations, and parted my land. 3 And they have cast lots for my people; and have given a boy for an harlot, and sold a girl for wine, that they might drink. 4 Yea, and what have ye to do with me, O Tyre, and Zidon, and all the coasts of Palestine? will ye render me a recompence? and if ye recompense me, swiftly and speedily will I return your recompence upon your own head; 5 Because ye have taken my silver and my gold, and have carried into your temples my goodly pleasant things: 6 The children also of Judah and the children of Jerusalem have ye sold unto the Grecians, that ye might remove them far from their border. 7 Behold, I will raise them out of the place whither ye have sold them, and will return your recompence upon your own head: 8 And I will sell your sons and your daughters into the hand of the children of Judah, and they shall sell them to the Sabeans, to a people far off: for the LORD hath spoken it.*[148]

Joel 3 begins with a list of atrocities committed against Israel. These atrocities are specifically cited as grounds for judgment. It lends back to an Abrahamic Covenant promise made in Genesis 12.

> *Genesis 12:1 Now the LORD had said unto Abram, Get thee out of thy country, and from thy kindred, and from thy father's house, unto a land that I will shew thee: 2 And I will make of thee a great nation, and I will bless thee, and make thy name great; and thou shalt be a blessing: 3 <u>And I will bless them that bless thee, and curse him that curseth thee</u>: and in thee shall all families of the earth be blessed.*[149]

One such blessing for those who bless His brethren is found in Revelation 19, which sees an invitation extended to participate in the marriage supper of the Lamb. Said marriage supper will occur on earth in the Millennial Kingdom.

> *Revelation 19:9 And he saith unto me, Write, Blessed are they which are called unto the marriage supper of the Lamb. And he saith unto me, These are the true sayings of God.*[150]

Those who are not blessed to receive an invitation are those who will have been guilty of cursing His brethren. Therefore, Matthew 25:41 refers to them as "cursed", and they are told to depart from Him into everlasting punishment.

The next verses of Joel 3 detail the willingness of the Gentile nations which have "cursed" Israel to gather together to fight against Jesus, as it will be Jesus who fights on behalf of His people.

> *Joel 3:9 Proclaim ye this among the Gentiles; Prepare war, wake up the mighty men, let all the men of war draw near; let them come up: 10 Beat your plowshares into swords and your pruninghooks into spears: let the weak say, I am strong. 11 Assemble yourselves, and come, all ye heathen, and gather yourselves together round about: thither cause thy mighty ones to come down, O LORD. 12 Let the heathen be wakened, and come up to the valley of Jehoshaphat: for there will I sit to judge all the heathen round about. 13 Put ye in the sickle, for the harvest is ripe: come, get you down; for the press is full, the fats overflow; for their wickedness is great. 14 Multitudes, multitudes in the valley of decision: for the day of the LORD is near in the valley of decision.*

The above verses are also linked to the Battle of Armageddon, which we know takes place at the Second Coming of Jesus Christ. The nations which gather at the end of the age for this battle do not actually fight in the Valley of Megiddo, otherwise known as the Kidron Valley. Rather, Megiddo is simply where they will initially gather for the battle of the "Great Day of God Almighty".

> *Revelation 16:12 And the sixth angel poured out his vial upon the great river Euphrates; and the water thereof was dried up, that the way of the kings of the east might be prepared. 13 And I saw three unclean spirits like frogs come out of the mouth of the dragon, and out of the mouth of the beast, and out of the mouth of the false prophet. 14 For they are the spirits of devils, working miracles, which go forth unto the kings of the earth and of the whole world, to gather them to the battle of that great day of God Almighty.*
> *15 Behold, I come as a thief. Blessed is he that watcheth, and keepeth his garments, lest he walk naked, and they see his shame. 16 And he gathered them together into a place called in the Hebrew tongue Armageddon.*[151]

It is after the nations gather and begin making their trek toward Jerusalem, toward the valley of decision, the Lord will roar from Zion and have His way with those armies which seek to defeat Him.

> *Joel 3:15 The sun and the moon shall be darkened, and the stars shall withdraw their shining. 16 The LORD also shall roar out of Zion, and utter his voice from Jerusalem; and the heavens and the earth shall shake: but the LORD will be the hope of his people, and the strength of the children of Israel. 17 So shall ye know that I am the LORD your God dwelling in Zion, my holy mountain: then shall Jerusalem be holy, and there shall no strangers pass through her any more.*

We can find additional details of the judgment of this day from other passages in the Old Testament. We will get to them in just a bit. First, we need to take a step back, because we are told even before the Lord judges the nations at Jerusalem, He will have saved the tents of Judah.

> *Zechariah 12:1 The burden of the word of the LORD for Israel, saith the LORD, which stretcheth forth the heavens, and layeth the foundation of the earth, and formeth the spirit of man within him. 2 Behold, I will make Jerusalem a cup of trembling unto all the people round about, when they shall be in the siege both against Judah and against Jerusalem. 3 And in that day will I make Jerusalem a burdensome stone for all people: all that burden themselves with it shall be cut in pieces, though all the people of the earth be gathered together against it. 4 In that day, saith the LORD, I will smite every horse with astonishment, and his rider with madness: and I will open mine eyes upon the house of Judah, and will smite every horse of the people with blindness. 5 And the governors of Judah shall say in their heart, The inhabitants of Jerusalem shall be my strength in the LORD of hosts their God. 6 In that day will I make the governors of Judah like an hearth of fire among the wood, and like a torch of fire in a sheaf; and they shall devour all the people round about, on the right hand and on the left: and Jerusalem shall be inhabited again in her own place, even in Jerusalem. 7 <u>The LORD also shall save the tents of Judah first</u>, that the glory of the house of David and the glory of the inhabitants of Jerusalem do not magnify themselves against Judah. 8 In that day shall the LORD defend the inhabitants of Jerusalem; and he that is feeble among them at that day shall be as David; and the house of David shall be as God, as the angel of the LORD before them. 9 <u>And it shall come to pass in that day, that I will seek to destroy all the nations that come against Jerusalem</u>.*[152]

In Zechariah 12:9, we see the lead-in to the judgment of the nations which was referenced in Joel 3 and Matthew 25. Just prior to that judgment, though, the Lord will have saved the tents of Judah, as we see in Zechariah 12:7. Why will Judah be dwelling in tents?

We are told in Leviticus 23 the feast of Tabernacles is a memorial of the 40 years the Israelites spent wandering in the desert after the Lord delivered them out of Egypt. During their 40 years in the desert, they lived in temporary dwellings or tents. At the midpoint of the 70th Week, those who witness the abomination of desolation referenced in both Daniel 9:27 and Matthew 24:15-22 will be forced to flee Jerusalem. Revelation 12 paints a specific picture of the flight of the remnant and of their supernatural protection by God during said flight. It also paints a picture of their continued protection through the end of the Week, which includes once again residing in temporary dwellings or tents in the wilderness. At the end of the remnant's 1260 days in the wilderness, also called a time, times, and half a time, they will be delivered by the Messiah they will have recognized and called upon for salvation. He will return to provide exactly that.

It is believed the Jews will seek shelter in Petra during this second half of Daniel's 70th Week. The ancient name for Petra is Bozrah. We find a clear picture of the Lord providing salvation for the remnant at Bozrah in the following passage.

> *Micah 2:12 I will surely assemble, O Jacob, all of thee; I will surely gather the remnant of Israel; I will put them together as the sheep of Bozrah, as the flock in the midst of their fold: they shall make great noise by reason of the multitude of men. 13 The breaker is come up before them: they have broken up, and have passed through the gate, and are gone out by it: and their king shall pass before them, and the LORD on the head of them.*[153]

When the Chief Shepherd shall appear, He will save His flock. Isaiah 63 also refers to the Lord's salvation of those who will be in Bozrah.

> *Isaiah 63:1 Who is this that cometh from Edom, with dyed garments from Bozrah? this that is glorious in his apparel, travelling in the greatness of his strength? I that speak in righteousness, mighty to save. 2 Wherefore art thou red in thine apparel, and thy garments like him that treadeth in the winefat? 3 I have trodden the winepress alone; and of the people there was none with me: for I will tread them in mine anger, and trample them in my fury; and their blood shall be sprinkled upon my garments, and I will stain all my raiment. 4 For the day of vengeance is in mine heart, and the year of my redeemed is come. 5 And I looked, and there was none to help; and I wondered that there was none to uphold: therefore mine own arm brought salvation unto me; and my fury, it upheld me. 6 And I will tread down the people in mine anger, and make them drunk in my fury, and I will bring down their strength to the earth.*[154]

From Edom, which is where Bozrah is located, the Lord Jesus Christ will tread the winepress of the wrath of Almighty God. Revelation 19 touches on Jesus's treading of the winepress, but Revelation 14 expresses this concept more fully. We will begin with the reference made in Revelation 19.

> *Revelation 19:11 And I saw heaven opened, and behold a white horse; and he that sat upon him was called Faithful and True, and in righteousness he doth judge and make war. 12 His eyes were as a flame of fire, and on his head were many crowns; and he had a name written, that no man knew, but he himself. 13 And he was clothed with a vesture dipped in blood: and his name is called The Word of God. 14 And the armies which were in heaven followed him upon white*

> *horses, clothed in fine linen, white and clean. 15 And out of his mouth goeth a sharp sword, that with it he should smite the nations: and he shall rule them with a rod of iron: and he treadeth the winepress of the fierceness and wrath of Almighty God.*

Revelation 14 gives us more specific detail which encompasses the whole of the judgment we have been talking about to this point.

> *Revelation 14:14 And I looked, and behold a white cloud, and upon the cloud one sat like unto the Son of man, having on his head a golden crown, and in his hand a sharp sickle. 16 And he that sat on the cloud thrust in his sickle on the earth; and the earth was reaped. 17 And another angel came out of the temple which is in heaven, he also having a sharp sickle. 18 And another angel came out from the altar, which had power over fire; and cried with a loud cry to him that had the sharp sickle, saying, Thrust in thy sharp sickle, and gather the clusters of the vine of the earth; for her grapes are fully ripe. 19 And the angel thrust in his sickle into the earth, and gathered the vine of the earth, and cast it into the great winepress of the wrath of God. 20 And the winepress was trodden without the city, and blood came out of the winepress, even unto the horse bridles, by the space of a thousand and six hundred furlongs.*[155]

One thousand and six hundred furlongs is the distance between Bozrah and Megiddo. All of those who stand against Israel, and more specifically against Jesus Christ, will be utterly laid waste. Thus, as Zechariah 12:7-9 tell us, the Lord will save the tents of Judah first, then judge all the nations.

Each of these passages of Scripture tell of the events which will occur on the Day of the Lord. Some simply give more detail or different details than others to paint a bigger picture. We will continue with the judgment aspect in just a bit, but before I get there I need to develop another idea which lends itself to the way in which Jesus will judge the nations. It deals with the concept of "light".

The Light of the World

Many of you may be familiar with the idea that Jesus is the Light of the World. Jesus makes this reference to Himself in John 8.

> *John 8:12 Then spake Jesus again unto them, saying, I am the light of the world: he that followeth me shall not walk in darkness, but shall have the light of life.*[156]

To understand this concept more fully, we need to understand the shared deity and divinity Jesus has with God. We also need to understand one important thing about God: God is light.

> *I John 1:5 This then is the message which we have heard of him, and declare unto you, that God is light, and in him is no darkness at all.*

From this, we understand a clear separation exists between light and darkness. They cannot comingle, whatsoever. This understanding lends to the following references made about our familial relationships with God, who is light.

> *John 1:12 But as many as received him, to them gave he power to become the sons of God, even to them that believe on his name:*[157]

> *I Thessalonians 5:5 Ye are all the children of light, and the children of the day: we are not of the night, nor of darkness.*[158]

Here is another point made about us being of the same light God is.

> *Mathew 5:14 Ye are the light of the world. A city that is set on an hill cannot be hid. 15 Neither do men light a candle, and put it under a bushel, but on a candlestick; and it giveth*

> *light unto all that are in the house. 16 Let your light so shine before men, that they may see your good works, and glorify your Father which is in heaven.*[159]

After we believe in Jesus, God puts His seal of approval on us. One of the ways in which this occurs is through the indwelling of the Holy Spirit. We are also moved from darkness into light.

> *I Peter 2:9 But ye are a chosen generation, a royal priesthood, an holy nation, a peculiar people; that ye should shew forth the praises of him who hath called you out of darkness into his marvellous light;*[160]

Again, all these things denote a distinct separation between light and darkness, and thus between belief and unbelief. It is thought "ordo ab chao" or "order out of chaos" is a New World Order phrase. It is not. God is the original author of "order out of chaos". Chaos is essentially what the word "darkness" translates to.

> *Genesis 1:1 In the beginning God created the heaven and the earth. 2 And the earth was without form, and void; and darkness was upon the face of the deep. And the Spirit of God moved upon the face of the waters. 3 And God said, Let there be light: and there was light. 4 And God saw the light, that it was good: and God divided the light from the darkness. 5 And God called the light Day, and the darkness he called Night. And the evening and the morning were the first day.*[161]

The very first thing the Bible tells us in Genesis 1:1 is God created everything. The rest of Genesis 1 describes the process by which that creation came about. The will of God exercised through the voice of God (the Word of God, Jesus Christ) brought everything into being. Genesis 1:5 is interesting where it says *"And God called the light Day, and the darkness he called Night"*. Doesn't it remind you of what Paul wrote in I Thessalonians 5?

> *I Thessalonians 5:5 Ye are all the children of light, and the children of the day: we are not of the night, nor of darkness.*

In Genesis 1:3, God said, *"Let there be light: and there was light"*. You may recall we are told in I John 1:5 that God is light. The very first thing God did when He began to create was lend a part of Himself to creation. He put His stamp of ownership on it from day one by giving it the characteristic of His very being – light.

When I consider this, I liken it to a painter putting his signature on his artwork when it's complete. But God put didn't put His signature on His creation when He was finished. Rather, He placed it on His creation from the very beginning. It is for this reason Paul wrote in Romans 1 about one's ability to observe creation and come to knowledge of the Creator.

> *Romans 1:20 For the invisible things of him from the creation of the world are clearly seen, being understood by the things that are made, even his eternal power and Godhead; so that they are without excuse:*[162]

"The invisible things of him" is a reference to His light. We must remember visible light was not created until Day Four when God created the sun, moon, and stars. What then was this light mentioned on Day One? God's eternal power and Godhead are observable in creation, because the very characteristic of God – light – was the foundation of creation. We do not just observe what He did. We observe Him through His handiwork. The concept of God's light being the foundation of His creation is expressed similarly in the idea that God's "Light of the World" is the foundation for the salvation of His greatest creation: mankind.

The Glorious Appearing

To this point, the "light and darkness" conversation has been one of a spiritual nature. However, there is an aspect of the person of God which also deals with light that is very literal. It is in the context of the glorious appearing of the Lord Jesus Christ. We anticipate the Second Coming to be a glorious appearing, but it is not the only one in the Bible. The Second Coming will be the glorious appearing of God in the person of the Son.

> *John 4:24 God is a Spirit: and they that worship him must worship him in spirit and in truth.*[163]

In John 14:6, we learn Jesus is the "truth". Thus, John 4:24 tells us to worship God in the person of the Father and in the person of the Son, by means of the person of the Spirit inside us. It's a trinity thing.

We have at least several references to God being a light to the children of Israel in the Old Testament: as a pillar of fire, as present in a cloud, as filling the tabernacle and temple, etc. There is not just a spiritual light associated with God, as Day One of creation shows. There is also a very literal light associated with God.

Before I get to how this light impacts the person of Jesus Christ, let's look at two of the revelations of the light, or glory, of God in the Old Testament. The glory of the Lord appeared in a cloud atop Mount Sinai (Exodus 19). It was also present to anoint the most holy in Solomon's temple (II Chronicles 7). In the former situation, the glory of the Lord appeared in a cloud so as not to destroy Moses when He was in God's presence. However, when the glory of the Lord filled Solomon's temple, there was no such barrier. For this reason, no one could enter the temple while the glory of the Lord was filling it, lest they be destroyed.

These differences of the appearance of the glory of the Lord in the Old Testament are also showcased in the New Testament with the first and second comings of Jesus Christ.

> *John 1:1 In the beginning was the Word, and the Word was with God, and the Word was God. 2 The same was in the beginning with God. 3 All things were made by him; and without him was not any thing made that was made. 4 In him was life; and the life was the light of men. 5 And the light shineth in darkness; and the darkness comprehended it not.[164]*

Jesus has always been God in the flesh. The difference at His first coming was His glory was tempered by His humanity. Thus, sinful mankind could look upon Him without being destroyed.

> *John 1:14 And the Word was made flesh, and dwelt among us, (and we beheld his glory, the glory as of the only begotten of the Father,) full of grace and truth.*

However, at His Second Coming, there will be no such barrier. The glory of the glorified Jesus Christ will burn away that which cannot stand in its presence: sin. Only the righteousness of God imparted through faith in Jesus Christ will be able to withstand.

> *Joel 3:16 The LORD also shall roar out of Zion, and utter his voice from Jerusalem; and the heavens and the earth shall shake: but the LORD will be the hope of his people, and the strength of the children of Israel.*

We are told the Lord, when He appears at the Second Coming, will "*roar out of Zion, and utter His voice from Jerusalem*". This is where the heavens will open and show the Lord coming forth with His heavenly armies, per Revelation 19:11-14. At that time, the heavens and the earth shall shake. Compare Joel 3:16 to the following verse from II Peter 3:

> *II Peter 3:10 But the day of the Lord will come as a thief in the night; in the which the heavens shall pass away with a great noise, and the elements shall melt with fervent heat, the earth also and the works that are therein shall be burned up.*[165]

Matthew 24 also refers to this event.

> *Matthew 24:29 Immediately after the tribulation of those days shall the sun be darkened, and the moon shall not give her light, and the stars shall fall from heaven, and the powers of the heavens shall be shaken: 30 And then shall appear the sign of the Son of man in heaven: and then shall all the tribes of the earth mourn, and they shall see the Son of man coming in the clouds of heaven with power and great glory. 35 Heaven and earth shall pass away, but my words shall not pass away.*[166]

Daniel 7 refers to the day of the Second Coming, as well.

> *Daniel 7:9 I beheld till the thrones were cast down, and the Ancient of days did sit, whose garment was white as snow, and the hair of his head like the pure wool: his throne was like the fiery flame, and his wheels as burning fire. 10 A fiery stream issued and came forth from before him: thousand thousands ministered unto him, and ten thousand times ten thousand stood before him: the judgment was set, and the books were opened.*[167]

What thrones are being cast down in Daniel 7:9? Those of the angelic host which have been given power over the nations since Babel.

> *Psalm 82:6 I have said, Ye are gods; and all of you are children of the most High. 7 But ye shall die like men, and fall like one of the princes. 8 Arise, O God, judge the earth: for thou shalt inherit all nations.*[168]

Psalm 82 is more than likely what Matthew 24:29's *"and the stars shall fall from heaven, and the powers of the heavens shall be shaken"* is a reference to.

What is Daniel 7:10 referring to when it says *"a fiery stream issued and came forth from before Him"*?

> *Isaiah 11:4 But with righteousness shall he judge the poor, and reprove with equity for the meek of the earth: and he shall smite the earth: with the rod of his mouth, and with the breath of his lips shall he slay the wicked.*[169]

> *Revelation 19:19 And I saw the beast, and the kings of the earth, and their armies, gathered together to make war against him that sat on the horse, and against his army. 20 And the beast was taken, and with him the false prophet that wrought miracles before him, with which he deceived them that had received the mark of the beast, and them that worshipped his image. These both were cast alive into a lake of fire burning with brimstone. 21 And the remnant were slain with the sword of him that sat upon the horse, which sword proceeded out of his mouth: and all the fowls were filled with their flesh.*[170]

> *II Thessalonians 2:8 And then shall that Wicked be revealed, whom the Lord shall consume with the spirit of his mouth, and shall destroy with the brightness of his coming:*[171]

> *Deuteronomy 4:24 For the* L<small>ORD</small> *thy God is a consuming fire, even a jealous God.*[172]

Judgment shall be made by the command which proceeds out of His mouth, along with the glory exuding from His physical presence, and everything in creation which is unrighteous will be destroyed. This is the day His feet will stand on the Mount of Olives. From this mount, He will judge the nations which came against His people, as we read about in Matthew 25, Joel 3, and Zechariah 12:9. Let's move to Zechariah 14 and continue discussing the judgment of the great day.

> *Zechariah 14:1 Behold, the day of the* L<small>ORD</small> *cometh, and thy spoil shall be divided in the midst of thee. 2 For I will gather all nations against Jerusalem to battle; and the city shall be taken, and the houses rifled, and the women ravished; and half of the city shall go forth into captivity, and the residue of the people shall not be cut off from the city. 3 Then shall the* L<small>ORD</small> *go forth, and fight against those nations, as when he fought in the day of battle. 4 And his feet shall stand in that day upon the mount of Olives, which is before Jerusalem on the east, and the mount of Olives shall cleave in the midst thereof toward the east and toward the west, and there shall be a very great valley; and half of the mountain shall remove toward the north, and half of it toward the south. 5 And ye shall flee to the valley of the mountains; for the valley of the mountains shall reach unto Azal: yea, ye shall flee, like as ye fled from before the earthquake in the days of Uzziah king of Judah: and the* L<small>ORD</small> *my God shall come, and all the saints with thee.*[173]

On judgment day, also referred to as the day of wrath or the Day of the Lord, the darkness vs. light conversation will have come full circle from day one of creation.

Zephaniah 1:15 That day is a day of wrath, a day of trouble and distress, a day of wasteness and desolation, <u>a day of darkness and gloominess, a day of clouds and thick darkness,</u> 16 A day of the trumpet and alarm against the fenced cities, and against the high towers. 17 And I will bring distress upon men, that they shall walk like blind men, because they have sinned against the L<small>ORD</small>*: and their blood shall be poured out as dust, and their flesh as the dung.*[174]

Joel 2:1 Blow ye the trumpet in Zion, and sound an alarm in my holy mountain: let all the inhabitants of the land tremble: for the day of the L<small>ORD</small> *cometh, for it is nigh at hand; 2 A <u>day of darkness and of gloominess, a day of clouds and of thick darkness,</u> as the morning spread upon the mountains: a great people and a strong; there hath not been ever the like, neither shall be any more after it, even to the years of many generations.*[175]

Amos 5:18 Woe unto you that desire the day of the L<small>ORD</small>*! to what end is it for you? <u>the day of the* L<small>ORD</small> *is darkness, and not light</u>. 19 As if a man did flee from a lion, and a bear met him; or went into the house, and leaned his hand on the wall, and a serpent bit him. 20 <u>Shall not the day of the* L<small>ORD</small> *be darkness, and not light? even very dark, and no brightness in it</u>?*[176]

But then… Jesus. Enter the Light of the World.

*Isaiah 60:1 Arise, shine; **<u>for thy light is come</u>**, and the glory of the* L<small>ORD</small> *is risen upon thee. 2 For, behold, <u>the darkness shall cover the earth, and gross darkness the people</u>: but the* L<small>ORD</small> *shall arise upon thee, and **<u>his glory shall be seen upon thee</u>**.*[177]

*Zechariah 14:6 And it shall come to pass in that day, that the light shall not be clear, nor dark: 7 But it shall be one day which shall be known to the LORD, not day, nor night: but it shall come to pass, that at evening time **it shall be light**.*

At evening time it shall be light

Where will all this darkness have come from in order that Jesus must destroy it with His light?

> *Revelation 16:10 And the fifth angel poured out his vial upon the seat of the beast; <u>and his kingdom was full of darkness</u>; and they gnawed their tongues for pain, 11 And blasphemed the God of heaven because of their pains and their sores, and repented not of their deeds.*[178]

If you've read through Revelation, you may have noticed the judgments bear much similarity to the 10 plagues from Exodus. One of those plagues regarded darkness falling over the land of Egypt. Not only was the darkness literal, it was also spiritual, so much so it could be felt. I believe this is exactly what kind of darkness will once again fall over the earth during this fifth vial judgment. Thus, the conditions will exist which cause the Day of the Lord to be a day of gloominess and thick darkness. There will be no light, likely except for the preserved remnant in Bozrah.

It is interesting to note we are given the time of day Jesus will return in Zechariah 14:7.

> *Zechariah 14:7 But it shall be one day which shall be known to the LORD, not day, nor night: but it shall come to pass, that at <u>evening time</u> it shall be light.*

The Day of the Lord will begin in the evening, just like the Hebrew day does. I've seen the Day of the Lord linked to the Feast of Trumpets due to what we are told about the darkness of the sun and moon on that day, as if a new moon or an eclipse of some sort will be involved. However, it is clear from all the verses above, an eclipse will not be the reason the sun and moon withdraw their shining. Rather, those things will occur because darkness will fill the land. At evening, darkness will cease from filling the land when the Light of the World makes His presence known.

The glory of the Lord will be seen by all. It will destroy the sin and wickedness which will prevail upon the earth in that day. It will put an end to the darkness. Thus, the Kingdom He will bring from heaven to earth will be established in total righteousness.

We can now circle back to the purposes for the 70 Weeks and see how they will find fulfillment on this Day of the Lord.

The 70 Weeks Completed

In Part Two of this study, I detailed the prophecy contained in Daniel 9:27. The verse characterizes the events which will occur at the beginning, midpoint, and end of the Week.

> *Daniel 9:27 And he shall confirm the covenant with many for one week: and in the midst of the week he shall cause the sacrifice and the oblation to cease, and for the overspreading of abominations he shall make it desolate, even until the consummation, and that determined shall be poured upon the desolate.*[179]

The end of the Week is marked by Jesus destroying the Antichrist, effectively putting an end to his reign of terror.

> *Daniel 11:36 And the king shall do according to his will; and he shall exalt himself, and magnify himself above every god, and shall speak marvellous things against the God of gods, and shall prosper till the indignation be accomplished: for that that is determined shall be done.*[180]

> *II Thessalonians 2:8b whom the Lord shall consume with the spirit of his mouth, and shall destroy with the brightness of his coming:*

> *Daniel 7:11 I beheld then because of the voice of the great words which the horn spake: I beheld even till the beast was slain, and his body destroyed, and given to the burning flame.*[181]

> *Revelation 19:20 And the beast was taken, and with him the false prophet that wrought miracles before him, with which he deceived them that had received the mark of the beast, and*

them that worshipped his image. These both were cast alive into a lake of fire burning with brimstone.

With the judgment of the nations and the destruction of the Antichrist, Daniel's 70th week will be complete. Thus, the purposes for the 70 Weeks will also be complete. Here is another look at what those purposes are.

Daniel 9:24 Seventy weeks are determined upon thy people and upon thy holy city, to finish the transgression, and to make an end of sins, and to make reconciliation for iniquity, and to bring in everlasting righteousness, and to seal up the vision and prophecy, and to anoint the most Holy.

We will now go through the purposes individually and see how they will be fulfilled with the Second Coming of Jesus Christ.

To finish the transgression

The first thing we need to be aware of regarding the 70 Weeks prophecy is that it regards "thy people" and "thy holy city". More specifically, the prophecy regards Israel and Jerusalem. Thus, the fulfillment of the prophecy will also regard Israel and Jerusalem. Let's begin with the first of the six purposes by taking another look at what Dr. Arnold Fruchtenbaum wrote.

> *Daniel was next told by Gabriel that the 70 sevens are to accomplish six purposes. The first is* ***to finish transgression.*** *The Hebrew word translated "to finish" means "to restrain firmly," "to restrain completely" or "to bring to completion." The Hebrew word translated "transgression" is a very strong word for sin and more literally means "to rebel." The Hebrew text has this word with the definite article, so literally it means "the transgression," or "the rebellion." The point is that some specific act of rebellion is finally going to be completely restrained and brought to an end. This act of rebellion or transgression is to come under complete control so that it will no longer flourish. Israel's apostasy is now to be firmly restrained, in keeping with a similar prediction in Isaiah 59:20.*

Dr. Fruchtenbaum said this transgression is a specific transgression. *"The point is that some specific act of rebellion is finally going to be completely restrained and brought to an end. This act of rebellion or transgression is to come under complete control so that it will no longer flourish."* What then is this specific transgression which will be ended by the appearance of Jesus Christ?

Romans 11 details this specific transgression, and I referenced it in Part One when talking about the dispensational aspect of the Battle of Gog and Magog. Israel's transgression which caused God to hide His face from her and turn it to the church was her rejection of His Messiah and Redeemer. After Israel rejected

Jesus and demanded His crucifixion, the New Covenant was born. Thus, the church age began. However, there will come a time when the church will be removed so God can return His focus to Israel and finish dealing with her. He will do so via the 70th Week. By the end of the Week, Israel will have corrected her monumental error in shunning Jesus Christ by recognizing He is, indeed, her true Messiah.

> *Matthew 23:39 For I say unto you, Ye shall not see me henceforth, till ye shall say, Blessed is he that cometh in the name of the Lord.*[182]

> *Hosea 5:15 I will go and return to my place, till they acknowledge their offence, and seek my face: in their affliction they will seek me early.*[183]

Although Israel must endure significant hardship before she comes to the knowledge Jesus is the Christ, the Son of the Living God, she will indeed come to such a conclusion.

> *Zechariah 13:6 And one shall say unto him, What are these wounds in thine hands? Then he shall answer, Those with which I was wounded in the house of my friends. 7 Awake, O sword, against my shepherd, and against the man that is my fellow, saith the LORD of hosts: smite the shepherd, and the sheep shall be scattered: and I will turn mine hand upon the little ones. 8 And it shall come to pass, that in all the land, saith the LORD, two parts therein shall be cut off and die; but the third shall be left therein. 9 And I will bring the third part through the fire, and will refine them as silver is refined, and will try them as gold is tried: they shall call on my name, and I will hear them: I will say, It is my people: and they shall say, The LORD is my God.*[184]

Dr. Fruchtenbaum ended that segment with a reference to Isaiah 59:20.

> *Isaiah 59:19 So shall they fear the name of the LORD from the west, and his glory from the rising of the sun. When the enemy shall come in like a flood, the Spirit of the LORD shall lift up a standard against him. 20 And the Redeemer shall come to Zion, and unto them that turn from transgression in Jacob, saith the LORD.*[185]

We see similar language about the Redeemer coming to Zion to save the faithful remnant in Joel 2 and Romans 11.

> *Joel 2:32 And it shall come to pass, that whosoever shall call on the name of the LORD shall be delivered: for in mount Zion and in Jerusalem shall be deliverance, as the LORD hath said, and in the remnant whom the LORD shall call.*[186]

> *Romans 11:26 And so all Israel shall be saved: as it is written, There shall come out of Sion the Deliverer, and shall turn away ungodliness from Jacob:*[187]

The transgression, which saw Israel rejecting her Messiah, will be finished when she recognizes and accepts her Messiah, calling upon Him for salvation.

To make an end of sins

The second purpose for the 70 Weeks is "to make an end of sins". This purpose corresponds with the first and is a result of having finished the transgression.

> *The second purpose of the 70 sevens is **to make an end of sins**. The Hebrew word translated "to make an end" literally means "to seal up" or "to shut up in prison." It means to be securely kept, locked up, not allowed to roam at random. The Hebrew word translated as "sins" literally means "to miss the mark." It refers to sins of daily life, rather than to one specific sin. Even these sins are to be put to an end and taken away. This, too, is quite in keeping with predictions by the prophets that proclaim that in the messianic kingdom, sinning would cease from Israel (Isaiah 27:9, Ezekiel 36:25-27, 37:23, Jeremiah 31:31-34).*

When Israel rejected her Messiah, she also rejected the New Covenant. When she recognizes her error, accepts Him, and calls upon Him, He will return. When He returns, it will be to make an end of her sins, which is what the New Covenant is designed to do.

> *Jeremiah 31:31 Behold, the days come, saith the LORD, that I will make a new covenant with the house of Israel, and with the house of Judah: 32 Not according to the covenant that I made with their fathers in the day that I took them by the hand to bring them out of the land of Egypt; which my covenant they brake, although I was an husband unto them, saith the LORD: 33 But this shall be the covenant that I will make with the house of Israel; After those days, saith the LORD, I will put my law in their inward parts, and write it in their hearts; and will be their God, and they shall be my people. 34 And they shall teach no more every man his neighbour, and every man his brother, saying, Know the*

> LORD: *for they shall all know me, from the least of them unto the greatest of them, saith the* LORD: *for I will forgive their iniquity, and I will remember their sin no more.*[188]

Thus, Israel will be righteous in the sight of God. She will move from only being the natural seed of Abraham...

> *Romans 9:6 Not as though the word of God hath taken none effect. For they are not all Israel, which are of Israel: 7 Neither, because they are the seed of Abraham, are they all children: but, In Isaac shall thy seed be called. 8 That is, They which are the children of the flesh, these are not the children of God: but the children of the promise are counted for the seed.*[189]

...to also being the spiritual seed of Abraham.

> *Galatians 3:6 Even as Abraham believed God, and it was accounted to him for righteousness. 7 Know ye therefore that they which are of faith, the same are the children of Abraham.*[190]

Israel will then be able to partake of all the Abrahamic covenant promises which were designed to reach ultimate fulfillment in the Kingdom and beyond.

> *Hebrews 11:8 By faith Abraham, when he was called to go out into a place which he should after receive for an inheritance, obeyed; and he went out, not knowing whither he went. 9 By faith he sojourned in the land of promise, as in a strange country, dwelling in tabernacles with Isaac and Jacob, the heirs with him of the same promise: 10 For he looked for a city which hath foundations, whose builder and maker is God.*

13 These all died in faith, not having received the promises, but having seen them afar off, and were persuaded of them, and embraced them, and confessed that they were strangers and pilgrims on the earth. 14 For they that say such things declare plainly that they seek a country. 15 And truly, if they had been mindful of that country from whence they came out, they might have had opportunity to have returned. 16 But now they desire a better country, that is, an heavenly: wherefore God is not ashamed to be called their God: for he hath prepared for them a city.[191]

Thus, by bringing Israel into the New Covenant, an end of sins will have been made.

To make reconciliation for iniquity

The third purpose for the 70 Weeks is "to make reconciliation for iniquity". This purpose is also related to the New Covenant.

> *The third purpose is **to make reconciliation for iniquity**. The Hebrew word translated "to make reconciliation" is "kaphar," which has the same root meaning as the word "kippur," as in Yom Kippur. The word "kaphar" literally means "to make atonement." The third purpose, then, is to make atonement in some way for iniquity. In fact, it is by means of this atonement that the first two purposes will also be accomplished, that of finishing the transgression and making an end of sins. The word translated "iniquity" refers to inward sin. This has sometimes been referred to as the sin nature, or perhaps a more common term among Jewish people would be yetzer hara," the evil inclination."*

Many people, including myself in the past, have been able to make a solid case for why the Second Coming of Jesus may occur on the Day of Atonement. It is especially easy to do when reading passages like this which seemingly make a connection with Yom Kippur. However, I believe the tie to atonement (kaphar/kippur) goes beyond the surface interpretation and into a deeper explanation.

The Hebrew word for "reconciliation" is "ū-lə-ḵap-pêr".[192] It is used only three times in the Old Testament: in Daniel 9:24, Numbers 8:19, and I Chronicles 6:49. The two references outside of Daniel regard the annual atonement made by the high priest for the sins of Israel. But there is a bit more to the story where Jesus is concerned. The way in which Daniel's 9:24's reconciliation for iniquity will be made steps far beyond the Old Testament priesthood sacrifice for sins offered on the Day of Atonement. After all, Jesus is not your average high priest.

Zechariah 6 contains a prophecy which is expounded upon in Hebrews 7. In Old Testament times, the offices of king and priest were always separate. Melchizedek, from Genesis 14, was a notable exception and held both offices. He is a type and shadow of Jesus Christ who will also hold the office of both King and Priest.

> *Zechariah 6:12 And speak unto him, saying, Thus speaketh the LORD of hosts, saying, Behold the man whose name is The BRANCH; and he shall grow up out of his place, and he shall build the temple of the LORD: 13 Even he shall build the temple of the LORD; and he shall bear the glory, and shall sit and rule upon his throne; and he shall be a priest upon his throne: and the counsel of peace shall be between them both.*[193]

As I mentioned, Hebrews 7 develops this idea even further. While I won't include the entire text of the chapter, I will point out key verses which explain this idea a bit more. The following verses regard Melchizedek, and as you read them, you will likely notice similarities between him and Jesus.

> *Hebrews 7:1 For this Melchisedec, king of Salem, priest of the most high God, who met Abraham returning from the slaughter of the kings, and blessed him; 2 To whom also Abraham gave a tenth part of all; first being by interpretation King of righteousness, and after that also King of Salem, which is, King of peace; 3 Without father, without mother, without descent, having neither beginning of days, nor end of life; but made like unto the Son of God; abideth a priest continually.*[194]

And regarding Jesus:

> *Hebrews 7:15 And it is yet far more evident: for that after the similitude of Melchisedec there ariseth another priest, 16 Who is made, not after the law of a carnal commandment, but after the power of an endless life. 17 For he testifieth, Thou art a priest for ever after the order of Melchisedec.*
>
> *22 By so much was Jesus made a surety of a better testament. 23 And they truly were many priests, because they were not suffered to continue by reason of death: 24 But this man, because he continueth ever, hath an unchangeable priesthood. 25 Wherefore he is able also to save them to the uttermost that come unto God by him, seeing he ever liveth to make intercession for them. 26 For such an high priest became us, who is holy, harmless, undefiled, separate from sinners, and made higher than the heavens; 27 Who needeth not daily, as those high priests, to offer up sacrifice, first for his own sins, and then for the people's: for this he did once, when he offered up himself. 28 For the law maketh men high priests which have infirmity; but the word of the oath, which was since the law, maketh the Son, who is consecrated for evermore.*

As our High Priest, Jesus makes intercession for us. He is the mediator of the New Covenant between God and man.

> *Hebrews 4:14 Seeing then that we have a great high priest, that is passed into the heavens, Jesus the Son of God, let us hold fast our profession. 15 For we have not an high priest which cannot be touched with the feeling of our infirmities; but was in all points tempted like as we are, yet without sin. 16 Let us therefore come boldly unto the throne of grace, that we may obtain mercy, and find grace to help in time of need.*[195]

Hebrews 9 and 10 are replete with Scripture to help us understand how Jesus has performed His office of High Priest. Just as it was the duty of the high priest to offer up atoning sacrifices for the sins of Israel once a year, Jesus offered Himself up as the final sacrifice for sin. After Him, there is no other.

> *Hebrews 9:22 And almost all things are by the law purged with blood; and without shedding of blood is no remission. 23 It was therefore necessary that the patterns of things in the heavens should be purified with these; but the heavenly things themselves with better sacrifices than these. 24 For Christ is not entered into the holy places made with hands, which are the figures of the true; but into heaven itself, now to appear in the presence of God for us: 25 Nor yet that he should offer himself often, as the high priest entereth into the holy place every year with blood of others; 26 For then must he often have suffered since the foundation of the world: but now once in the end of the world hath he appeared to put away sin by the sacrifice of himself. 27 And as it is appointed unto men once to die, but after this the judgment: 28 So Christ was once offered to bear the sins of many; and unto them that look for him shall he appear the second time without sin unto salvation.[196]*

> *Hebrews 10:9 Then said he, Lo, I come to do thy will, O God. He taketh away the first, that he may establish the second. 10 By the which will we are sanctified through the offering of the body of Jesus Christ once for all. 11 And every priest standeth daily ministering and offering oftentimes the same sacrifices, which can never take away sins: 12 But this man, after he had offered one sacrifice for sins for ever, sat down on the right hand of God; 13 From henceforth expecting till his enemies be made his footstool. 14 For by one offering he hath perfected for ever them that are sanctified.[197]*

Unlike Old Testament times, the sacrifice of Jesus Christ did not occur on the Day of Atonement. In Part Three – the Feasts of the Lord, I discussed how the Day of Atonement was fulfilled in the person of Jesus Christ when He was baptized on that day. It was during His baptism Jesus identified Himself with sinful mankind, even though He had no sin. He began the ministry which would result in Him paying the penalty of our sins, which is death (Romans 6:23). Jesus was selected by God, just as the scapegoat had been in ancient times, to bear the sins of the world. His sacrifice would be complete roughly three and a half years later when He laid His life down on the cross on Passover.

> *Colossians 2:14 Blotting out the handwriting of ordinances that was against us, which was contrary to us, and took it out of the way, nailing it to his cross;*[198]

Jesus's death on the cross and His subsequent burial and resurrection are the three components of the Gospel message.

> *I Corinthians 15:1 Moreover, brethren, I declare unto you the gospel which I preached unto you, which also ye have received, and wherein ye stand; 2 By which also ye are saved, if ye keep in memory what I preached unto you, unless ye have believed in vain. 3 For I delivered unto you first of all that which I also received, how that Christ died for our sins according to the scriptures; 4 And that he was buried, and that he rose again the third day according to the scriptures:*[199]

When Israel understands whom her Messiah is, she will cry out for Him. He will return and gift her with a New Covenant relationship, as described in Jeremiah 31:31-34. This also lends itself to Israel understanding what she did to her Messiah. For that, she will mourn.

> *Zechariah 12:10 And I will pour upon the house of David, and upon the inhabitants of Jerusalem, the spirit of grace and of supplications: and they shall look upon me whom they have pierced, and they shall mourn for him, as one mourneth for his only son, and shall be in bitterness for him, as one that is in bitterness for his firstborn.*
>
> *Revelation 1:7 Behold, he cometh with clouds; and every eye shall see him, and they also which pierced him: and all kindreds of the earth shall wail because of him. Even so, Amen.*

Because Israel does not accept Jesus as her Messiah, she does not understand final atonement has been made. Therefore, she desires a third temple to resume the sacrificial system which has been absent for almost 2000 years. This does not bode well for her.

> *Hebrews 10:29 Of how much sorer punishment, suppose ye, shall he be thought worthy, who hath trodden under foot the Son of God, and hath counted the blood of the covenant, wherewith he was sanctified, an unholy thing, and hath done despite unto the Spirit of grace? 30 For we know him that hath said, Vengeance belongeth unto me, I will recompense, saith the Lord. And again, The Lord shall judge his people. 31 It is a fearful thing to fall into the hands of the living God.*[200]

It is easy to attach some sort of final judgment to this third purpose for the 70 Weeks, considering it regards atonement. However, since the purposes for the Week (at least so far) regard Israel and her salvation, I believe it has more to do with her understanding that final reconciliation has already been made. She will be reconciled to God the Father through the mediator Christ Jesus into the New Covenant. Israel cannot atone for her own iniquity. No one can atone for their own iniquity, which is why Jesus had to do it for us. Israel has not accepted that yet, but she will. Only then can the reconciliation which has already been made for iniquity be applied to her account.

To bring in everlasting righteousness

The fourth purpose for the 70 Weeks of Daniel is "to bring in everlasting righteousness". This purpose specifically relates to the Kingdom.

> *The fourth purpose of the 70 sevens is **to bring in everlasting righteousness.** More literally this could be translated "to bring in an age of righteousness," since the Hebrew "olam" is better translated as "age" rather than as "everlasting." This age of righteousness is to be the messianic kingdom spoken of in the Prophets (Isaiah 1:26, 11:2-5, 32:17; Jeremiah 23:5-6, 33:15-18). It is this very age that Daniel had been expecting to see established after the 70 years of captivity, but now he is told that will only be after the 490-year period.*

When I began Part Four of this end times timeline, I included the verse which got me interested in the study of the Day of the Lord: II Timothy 4:1.

> *II Timothy 4:1 I charge thee therefore before God, and the Lord Jesus Christ, who shall judge the quick and the dead at his appearing and his kingdom;*

I wrote about the one day in which judgment of the unrighteous will occur, leaving the righteous to enter His Kingdom. To explain this concept more fully, we need to look at some passages in Daniel which discuss the empires of old, as well as the final empire which will have no end. We will begin in Daniel 2 with Nebuchadnezzar's dream and Daniel's interpretation thereof.

> *Daniel 2:31 Thou, O king, sawest, and behold a great image. This great image, whose brightness was excellent, stood before thee; and the form thereof was terrible. 32 This*

> *image's head was of fine gold, his breast and his arms of silver, his belly and his thighs of brass, 33 His legs of iron, his feet part of iron and part of clay. 34 Thou sawest till that a stone was cut out without hands, which smote the image upon his feet that were of iron and clay, and brake them to pieces. 35 Then was the iron, the clay, the brass, the silver, and the gold, broken to pieces together, and became like the chaff of the summer threshingfloors; and the wind carried them away, that no place was found for them: and the stone that smote the image became a great mountain, and filled the whole earth.*[201]

Nebuchadnezzar had a dream of a statue wherein the body parts were represented by different materials: a head of gold, chest and arms of silver, belly and thighs of bronze, legs of iron, and feet of iron and clay. The dream continued until a stone not made of human hands dashed the feet of iron and clay into pieces, destroying them. Afterward, the rest of the statue was destroyed and dispersed like chaff on a threshing floor, carried away by the wind. Then, the stone which destroyed the statue filled the whole earth.

Nebuchadnezzar had no idea what the dream meant, but it troubled him. He sought counsel regarding its interpretation, and only Daniel could tell him.

> *Daniel 2:36 This is the dream; and we will tell the interpretation thereof before the king. 37 Thou, O king, art a king of kings: for the God of heaven hath given thee a kingdom, power, and strength, and glory. 38 And wheresoever the children of men dwell, the beasts of the field and the fowls of the heaven hath he given into thine hand, and hath made thee ruler over them all. Thou art this head of gold. 39 And after thee shall arise another kingdom inferior to thee, and another third kingdom of brass, which*

shall bear rule over all the earth. 40 And the fourth kingdom shall be strong as iron: forasmuch as iron breaketh in pieces and subdueth all things: and as iron that breaketh all these, shall it break in pieces and bruise. 41 And whereas thou sawest the feet and toes, part of potters' clay, and part of iron, the kingdom shall be divided; but there shall be in it of the strength of the iron, forasmuch as thou sawest the iron mixed with miry clay. 42 And as the toes of the feet were part of iron, and part of clay, so the kingdom shall be partly strong, and partly broken. 43 And whereas thou sawest iron mixed with miry clay, they shall mingle themselves with the seed of men: but they shall not cleave one to another, even as iron is not mixed with clay. 44 And in the days of these kings shall the God of heaven set up a kingdom, which shall never be destroyed: and the kingdom shall not be left to other people, but it shall break in pieces and consume all these kingdoms, and it shall stand for ever. 45 Forasmuch as thou sawest that the stone was cut out of the mountain without hands, and that it brake in pieces the iron, the brass, the clay, the silver, and the gold; the great God hath made known to the king what shall come to pass hereafter: and the dream is certain, and the interpretation thereof sure.

The head of bronze represented Nebuchadnezzar. More specifically, the head represented the empire which Nebuchadnezzar ruled: the Babylonian Empire. The chest and arms of silver represented the empire which would overcome Babylon and rule afterward. Around 538 B.C., Cyrus the Great of the Medo-Persian Empire defeated the Babylonian Empire, thus ending Israel's Babylonian Captivity and allowing her to return to her land. As a side note, it was Cyrus who allowed Israel to rebuild her temple after she returned from Babylon.

The belly and thighs of brass represented the empire which would overcome, and thus succeed, the Medo-Persian Empire, which was the Greek Empire. The fourth division of building materials represented the empire which would succeed the Greeks. This was the Roman Empire. Just as there were two legs on Nebuchadnezzar's statue, the Roman Empire had two "legs", which were its Eastern and Western divisions.

The final portion of building materials on the statue were found in the feet, which were composed of iron mixed with miry clay. Daniel noted there would be division within this final empire. Being composed of iron and clay, it will be partly strong and partly broken. It is thought the feet, which contain 10 toes, might be a link to the 10 kings which give power to the beast in the last days. It is also thought the final empire will be a revived Roman Empire of sorts, due to the legs being composed of iron, just as the feet were, in part. However, discussion of the origins of the final empire is outside the scope of this study.

It is important to note the order of empires begins with the most precious of all metals, but also the most malleable. Silver is less precious, but harder to bend or break. Brass is yet less precious than silver, but it is harder than silver. Finally, iron is the hardest of the metals but the least precious. That the final empire will be composed in part of iron and all its strength, yet mixed with clay which is easily breakable, is a testament to Daniel's interpretation of the division within the final empire. However, none of those metals or materials, regardless of their value or strength, will stand a chance against the stone which will dash them all to pieces.

> *Psalm 118:22 The stone which the builders refused is become the head stone of the corner. 23 This is the LORD's doing; it is marvellous in our eyes.*[202]

I Peter 2:4 To whom coming, as unto a living stone, disallowed indeed of men, but chosen of God, and precious,[203]

Ephesians 2:20 And are built upon the foundation of the apostles and prophets, Jesus Christ himself being the chief corner stone;[204]

The stone in Nebuchadnezzar's dream which shall dash the other empires to pieces and establish a kingdom throughout the whole of the earth is none other than Jesus Christ, Himself.

Daniel 4:3 How great are his signs! and how mighty are his wonders! his kingdom is an everlasting kingdom, and his dominion is from generation to generation.[205]

The underlying premise here is that each kingdom lasts until the one which overtakes it begins. Thus, the first day of the latter is the last day of former. This concept is also expressed in Daniel 7, which contains another dream of empires. This time, the dream is not Nebuchadnezzar's. It is Daniel's.

Daniel 7:1 In the first year of Belshazzar king of Babylon Daniel had a dream and visions of his head upon his bed: then he wrote the dream, and told the sum of the matters. 2 Daniel spake and said, I saw in my vision by night, and, behold, the four winds of the heaven strove upon the great sea. 3 And four great beasts came up from the sea, diverse one from another. 4 The first was like a lion, and had eagle's wings: I beheld till the wings thereof were plucked, and it was lifted up from the earth, and made stand upon the feet as a man, and a man's heart was given to it. 5 And behold another beast, a second, like to a bear, and it raised up itself on one side, and it had three ribs in the mouth of it between the teeth of it: and they said thus unto it, Arise, devour much flesh. 6 After this I beheld, and lo another, like a leopard, which had upon the back of it four wings of a fowl; the beast had also four heads; and dominion was given to it. 7 After this I saw in the night visions, and behold a fourth beast, dreadful and terrible, and strong exceedingly; and it had great iron teeth: it devoured and brake in pieces, and stamped the residue with the feet of it: and it was diverse from all the beasts that were before it; and it had ten horns. 8 I considered the horns, and, behold, there came up among them another little horn, before whom there were three of the first horns plucked up by the roots: and, behold, in this horn were eyes like the eyes of man, and a mouth speaking great things. 9 I beheld till the thrones were cast down, and the Ancient of days did sit, whose garment was white as snow, and the hair of his head like the pure wool: his throne was like the fiery flame, and his wheels as burning fire. 10 A fiery stream issued and came forth from before him: thousand thousands ministered unto him, and ten thousand times ten thousand stood before him: the judgment was set, and the books were opened. 11 I beheld then because of the voice of the great words which the horn spake: I beheld even till the beast was slain, and his body destroyed, and given to the burning flame.[206]

In Daniel's dream, he saw four beasts: a lion with eagle's wings; a bear with three ribs in its mouth; a leopard with four wings and four heads; and, a diverse beast with iron teeth and 10 horns. This dream represents the same empires which were in view in Nebuchadnezzar's dream in Daniel 2. The lion with eagle's wings represented Babylon. The bear with the three ribs in its mouth represented the Medo-Persians. The leopard with four wings and four heads represented Greece. Finally, the fourth beast which was diverse and had 10 horns represented the Romans. However, there is more to Daniel's dream. Regarding the fourth beast, Daniel saw a little horn rise among the 10, plucking up three as it went. This little horn is described as having eyes like a man and a mouth speaking great things.

    Daniel's dream continued as he saw the thrones of the angelic host, who had been given power over the nations since the time of Babel, cast down when the Ancient of Days returned to judge. Judgment was concluded when the body of the little horn which had spoken the great things was destroyed and given over to the burning flame. This little horn speaking great things represents the Antichrist. The kingdom which begins when the Antichrist's is destroyed will be the one which lasts forever.

The Prophesied Kingdom

The everlasting Kingdom which would be given to the Son to rule was prophesied in the Old Testament. That this everlasting Kingdom would be established after the judgment of the nations was also prophesied.

> *Psalm 2:7 I will declare the decree: the LORD hath said unto me, Thou art my Son; this day have I begotten thee. 8 Ask of me, and I shall give thee the heathen for thine inheritance, and the uttermost parts of the earth for thy possession. 9 Thou shalt break them with a rod of iron; thou shalt dash them in pieces like a potter's vessel. 10 Be wise now therefore, O ye kings: be instructed, ye judges of the earth. 11 Serve the LORD with fear, and rejoice with trembling. 12 Kiss the Son, lest he be angry, and ye perish from the way, when his wrath is kindled but a little. Blessed are all they that put their trust in him.*[207]

In the interim between His ascension and His return to earth to bring His Kingdom, Jesus is in heaven seated at the right hand of the Father. That He is seated is a testament to His finished work on the cross. In heaven, Jesus awaits the time appointed whereupon He will return to earth, put an end to the reign of the Antichrist, and begin to rule the Kingdom which has been promised to Him.

> *Hebrews 10:12 But this man, after he had offered one sacrifice for sins for ever, sat down on the right hand of God; 13 From henceforth expecting till his enemies be made his footstool.*[208]

That Jesus had been promised an earthly Kingdom to rule was not unknown to Satan. For this reason, Satan took Jesus to a high place and showed Him all the kingdoms of the world. Satan promised to give Jesus rule over all of them if Jesus would bow down and worship him. Jesus did not take the bait.

> *Matthew 4:8 Again, the devil taketh him up into an exceeding high mountain, and sheweth him all the kingdoms of the world, and the glory of them; 9 And saith unto him, All these things will I give thee, if thou wilt fall down and worship me. 10 Then saith Jesus unto him, Get thee hence, Satan: for it is written, Thou shalt worship the Lord thy God, and him only shalt thou serve.*[209]

The temptation here was to bypass the waiting period, to forgo the appointed time which God has ordained for Jesus to rightfully rule, and to give into immediate gratification. Satan's temptation was unsuccessful, and he was forced to flee from Jesus when given the command to do so.

There are many other prophesies in the Old and New Testaments which refer to a time when Jesus will reign. Below are just a few.

> *Micah 5:2 But thou, Bethlehem Ephratah, though thou be little among the thousands of Judah, yet out of thee shall he come forth unto me that is to be ruler in Israel; whose goings forth have been from of old, from everlasting.*[210]

> *Isaiah 9:6 For unto us a child is born, unto us a son is given: and the government shall be upon his shoulder: and his name shall be called Wonderful, Counsellor, The mighty God, The everlasting Father, The Prince of Peace. 7 Of the increase of his government and peace there shall be no end, upon the throne of David, and upon his kingdom, to order it, and to establish it with judgment and with justice from henceforth even for ever. The zeal of the* LORD *of hosts will perform this.*[211]

> *Isaiah 16:5 And in mercy shall the throne be established: and he shall sit upon it in truth in the tabernacle of David, judging, and seeking judgment, and hasting righteousness.*[212]
>
> *Luke 1:32 He shall be great, and shall be called the Son of the Highest: and the Lord God shall give unto him the throne of his father David: 33 And he shall reign over the house of Jacob for ever; and of his kingdom there shall be no end.*[213]

While His reign will be everlasting, the fifth purpose of the 70 Weeks of Daniel is to "bring in [an age of] righteousness". This is referred to as the Millennial Kingdom, where Jesus will bring the Kingdom from heaven to earth and rule and reign for 1000 years.

> *Revelation 19:6 Blessed and holy is he that hath part in the first resurrection: on such the second death hath no power, but they shall be priests of God and of Christ, and shall reign with him a thousand years.*[214]

The Kingdom on earth will be established in righteousness, for all the wicked will have been judged and removed from the earth upon His return.

> *Isaiah 1:26 And I will restore thy judges as at the first, and thy counsellors as at the beginning: afterward thou shalt be called, The city of righteousness, the faithful city. 27 Zion shall be redeemed with judgment, and her converts with righteousness. 28 And the destruction of the transgressors and of the sinners shall be together, and they that forsake the LORD shall be consumed.*[215]
>
> *Isaiah 32:16 Then judgment shall dwell in the wilderness, and righteousness remain in the fruitful field. 17 And the work of righteousness shall be peace; and the effect of righteousness quietness and assurance for ever.*[216]

> *Jeremiah 32:5 Behold, the days come, saith the LORD, that I will raise unto David a righteous Branch, and a King shall reign and prosper, and shall execute judgment and justice in the earth. 6 In his days Judah shall be saved, and Israel shall dwell safely: and this is his name whereby he shall be called, THE LORD OUR RIGHTEOUSNESS.*[217]

> *Isaiah 61:10 I will greatly rejoice in the LORD, my soul shall be joyful in my God; for he hath clothed me with the garments of salvation, he hath covered me with the robe of righteousness, as a bridegroom decketh himself with ornaments, and as a bride adorneth herself with her jewels. 11 For as the earth bringeth forth her bud, and as the garden causeth the things that are sown in it to spring forth; so the Lord GOD will cause righteousness and praise to spring forth before all the nations.*[218]

Jesus Christ will return to judge sin and wickedness by bringing His Kingdom to earth. His Kingdom will put an end to the one which will reign on earth at that time, which is the kingdom of the Antichrist. It will be just as Daniel 2 and 7 prophesied. The everlasting Kingdom will come to earth, and an age of righteousness will be established. The Day of the Lord might begin with judgment, but it will end with all who are still alive being declared fit to enter His Kingdom.

> *II Peter 3:8 But, beloved, be not ignorant of this one thing, that one day is with the Lord as a thousand years, and a thousand years as one day.*[219]

The idea expressed in II Peter 3:8 parallels the seven days of creation wherein God created the heavens and the earth in six days and rested on the seventh. Six thousand years of history will have been accomplished, and the seven thousandth year will be our sabbath rest in the Lord's Millennial Kingdom. Thus, the establishment of an age of righteousness will have been fulfilled.

To seal up vision and prophecy

The fifth purpose of the 70 Weeks of Daniel is "to seal up the vision and prophecy".

> *The fifth purpose is **to seal up vision and prophecy.** Here Daniel used a word which means "to shut up." So "to seal up" means to cause a cessation or to completely fulfill. Thus, vision and prophecy are to be completely fulfilled." Vision" is a reference to oral prophecy, while "prophecy" refers to written prophecy. Both oral and written prophecy will cease with the final fulfillment of all revelations.*

Bible prophecy is the tool by which we measure the lateness of the prophetic hour. What exactly does that mean? What is the prophetic hour which we are attempting to determine the lateness of? The answer to those questions is revealed when we understand what we are truly studying when we study Bible prophecy.

> *Revelation 19:10 And I fell at his feet to worship him. And he said unto me, See thou do it not: I am thy fellowservant, and of thy brethren that have the testimony of Jesus: worship God: <u>for the testimony of Jesus is the spirit of prophecy.</u>*[220]

When we study Bible prophecy, we are studying the testimony of Jesus Christ. The testimony of Jesus Christ includes all the events which will lead to a singular, much anticipated event: His Second Coming.

While there is no new prophecy currently being added to the Bible, there are many prophecies about Jesus which have not yet been fulfilled. However, there will come a point at which all written and oral prophecy will cease – when He returns. Why will prophecy cease? Because everything which has been prophesied, up to and including the revelation of Jesus Christ, will have been fulfilled. There will be nothing new to prophesy about, because the Person of whom prophecy testifies will be here with us. At the Second Coming, all prophecy will be sealed, consummated, or fulfilled. Afterward, we will be experiencing events in real-time right along with Jesus Christ.

To anoint the most holy

The final purpose of the 70 Weeks of Daniel is "to anoint the most holy".

> *The final purpose of the 70 sevens is **to anoint the most holy.** A better translation here would be "to anoint a most holy place." This is a reference to the Jewish temple which is to be rebuilt when Messiah comes. It refers to the same temple that Daniel's contemporary, Ezekiel, described in great detail (Ezekiel 40-48)."*

The anointing of the mostly holy is a reference to the presence of the glory of God in the temple. We have Biblical evidence of the anointing of the most holy in both the first and second temples, and as we will see, the future anointing of the most holy appears to be a combination of both. Let's begin by looking at how the first temple was anointed by the presence of God.

> *II Chronicles 5:1 Thus all the work that Solomon made for the house of the LORD was finished: and Solomon brought in all the things that David his father had dedicated; and the silver, and the gold, and all the instruments, put he among the treasures of the house of God. Then Solomon assembled the elders of Israel, and all the heads of the tribes, the chief of the fathers of the children of Israel, unto Jerusalem, to bring up the ark of the covenant of the LORD out of the city of David, which is Zion. 3 Wherefore all the men of Israel assembled themselves unto the king in the feast which was in the seventh month.[221]*

> *II Chronicles 7:1 Now when Solomon had made an end of praying, the fire came down from heaven, and consumed the burnt offering and the sacrifices; and the glory of the LORD filled the house. 2 And the priests could not enter into the*

> *house of the LORD, because the glory of the LORD had filled the LORD's house.*[222]

After Solomon finished construction of the first temple, a feast was held to dedicate the house to the Lord. At the end of the feast, which included many thousands of sacrifices, fire came down from heaven and consumed said sacrifices, declaring their acceptance by God. At the same time, the glory of the Lord filled the temple. No one could enter the temple while the glory of the Lord was filling it, lest they be killed by gazing upon it. The glory of the Lord filling the house of the Lord is what we refer to as "the anointing of the most holy".

Solomon's temple was destroyed in 588 B.C. when Jerusalem was sacked during the Babylonian Captivity. I will discuss this event in greater detail in Part Five of this study. A temple did not exist again until after the Captivity ended. The Medo-Persians conquered the Babylonian Empire around 538 B.C., led by Cyrus the Great. Cyrus allowed Israel to return home and gave the go-ahead for the temple to be rebuilt. Even so, the temple which was rebuilt lacked the luster and the grandeur of the first temple. It would, however, bear a greater glory than the first. The prophet Haggai tells us as much.

> *Haggai 2:1 In the seventh month, in the one and twentieth day of the month, came the word of the LORD by the prophet Haggai, saying, 2 Speak now to Zerubbabel the son of Shealtiel, governor of Judah, and to Joshua the son of Josedech, the high priest, and to the residue of the people, saying, 3 Who is left among you that saw this house in her first glory? and how do ye see it now? is it not in your eyes in comparison of it as nothing? 4 Yet now be strong, O Zerubbabel, saith the LORD; and be strong, O Joshua, son of Josedech, the high priest; and be strong, all ye people of the land, saith the LORD, and work: for I am with you, saith the*

> LORD *of hosts: 5 According to the word that I covenanted with you when ye came out of Egypt, so my spirit remaineth among you: fear ye not. 6 For thus saith the* LORD *of hosts; Yet once, it is a little while, and I will shake the heavens, and the earth, and the sea, and the dry land; 7 And I will shake all nations, and the desire of all nations shall come: and I will fill this house with glory, saith the* LORD *of hosts. 8 The silver is mine, and the gold is mine, saith the* LORD *of hosts. 9 The glory of this latter house shall be greater than of the former, saith the* LORD *of hosts: and in this place will I give peace, saith the* LORD *of hosts.*[223]

Haggai 2:3 tells us those who had been alive to see the first temple would gaze upon the second and realize it fell short of the magnificence of Solomon's temple. Even so, Haggai 2:9 tells us the glory of the second house would be greater than that of the first. How could that be? The answer lies in Haggai 2:7.

> *and the desire of all nations shall come: and I will fill this house with glory*

What does that mean?

The second temple would stand until Jerusalem was once again sacked and destroyed by Roman soldiers in 70 A.D. This temple would be the one which existed when Jesus walked the earth during His first coming. It would be the very same temple which saw Him preaching and teaching the multitudes. But Jesus's first visit to the temple would be when He was just a few days old. Eight, to be precise.

> *Luke 2:21 And when eight days were accomplished for the circumcising of the child, his name was called* JESUS, *which was so named of the angel before he was conceived in the womb. 22 And when the days of her purification according*

to the law of Moses were accomplished, they brought him to Jerusalem, to present him to the Lord; 23 (As it is written in the law of the LORD, Every male that openeth the womb shall be called holy to the Lord;) 24 And to offer a sacrifice according to that which is said in the law of the Lord, A pair of turtledoves, or two young pigeons. 25 And, behold, there was a man in Jerusalem, whose name was Simeon; and the same man was just and devout, waiting for the consolation of Israel: and the Holy Ghost was upon him. 26 And it was revealed unto him by the Holy Ghost, that he should not see death, before he had seen the Lord's Christ. 27 And he came by the Spirit into the temple: and when the parents brought in the child Jesus, to do for him after the custom of the law, 28 Then took he him up in his arms, and blessed God, and said, 29 Lord, now lettest thou thy servant depart in peace, according to thy word: 30 For mine eyes have seen thy salvation, 31 Which thou hast prepared before the face of all people; 32 A light to lighten the Gentiles, and the glory of thy people Israel. 33 And Joseph and his mother marvelled at those things which were spoken of him. 34 And Simeon blessed them, and said unto Mary his mother, Behold, this child is set for the fall and rising again of many in Israel; and for a sign which shall be spoken against; 35 (Yea, a sword shall pierce through thy own soul also,) that the thoughts of many hearts may be revealed.[224]

Luke 2 tells of the first time the glory of the Lord would anoint the temple. There would be other times which were written about in the Gospels. Even though the shekinah did not anoint the second temple like it did the first temple in II Chronicles 7, the physical person of Jesus Christ, who shares the Godhead with the Father, did. Thus, Haggai's prophecy was fulfilled. The desire of all nations came and filled the house with His glory.

> *John 1:14 And the Word was made flesh, and dwelt among us, (and we beheld his glory, the glory as of the only begotten of the Father,) full of grace and truth.*

That there will be another time when the anointing of the most holy occurs is espoused within this final purpose for the 70 Weeks. Thus, it mandates the existence of another temple which the glory of the Lord can enter. We know from Daniel 9:27 and Revelation 11, another temple will indeed be built during the 70th Week. There is never a destruction of this "tribulation temple" mentioned in the Bible, and we know from Ezekiel 40-48 a temple will exist in the Millennial Kingdom. Many people point to Zechariah 6 to show how the Lord will build a temple when He returns, thus differentiating the Millennial Temple from the tribulation temple. Let's look at the text to see if that is what is intended.

> *Zechariah 6:12 And speak unto him, saying, Thus speaketh the LORD of hosts, saying, Behold the man whose name is The BRANCH; and he shall grow up out of his place, and he shall build the temple of the LORD: 13 Even he shall build the temple of the LORD; and he shall bear the glory, and shall sit and rule upon his throne; and he shall be a priest upon his throne: and the counsel of peace shall be between them both.[225]*

The context of these verses regards the combined office of king and priest, which is unique because they were always held by two different people. The exceptions to this rule are Melchizedek and Jesus Christ. I wrote about this when discussing the third purpose for the 70 Weeks, which is to make reconciliation for iniquity. The temple which the Lord will build, combining the offices of King and Priest, regards Isaiah 53 and Jesus's role as the "suffering servant". This led to Him being our High Priest.

Isaiah 53:1 Who hath believed our report? and to whom is the arm of the L*ORD revealed? 2 For he shall grow up before him as a tender plant, and as a root out of a dry ground: he hath no form nor comeliness; and when we shall see him, there is no beauty that we should desire him. 3 He is despised and rejected of men; a man of sorrows, and acquainted with grief: and we hid as it were our faces from him; he was despised, and we esteemed him not. 4 Surely he hath borne our griefs, and carried our sorrows: yet we did esteem him stricken, smitten of God, and afflicted. 5 But he was wounded for our transgressions, he was bruised for our iniquities: the chastisement of our peace was upon him; and with his stripes we are healed. 6 All we like sheep have gone astray; we have turned every one to his own way; and the* L*ORD hath laid on him the iniquity of us all. 7 He was oppressed, and he was afflicted, yet he opened not his mouth: he is brought as a lamb to the slaughter, and as a sheep before her shearers is dumb, so he openeth not his mouth. 8 He was taken from prison and from judgment: and who shall declare his generation? for he was cut off out of the land of the living: for the transgression of my people was he stricken. 9 And he made his grave with the wicked, and with the rich in his death; because he had done no violence, neither was any deceit in his mouth. 10 Yet it pleased the* L*ORD to bruise him; he hath put him to grief: when thou shalt make his soul an offering for sin, he shall see his seed, he shall prolong his days, and the pleasure of the* L*ORD shall prosper in his hand. 11 He shall see of the travail of his soul, and shall be satisfied: by his knowledge shall my righteous servant justify many; for he shall bear their iniquities. 12 Therefore will I divide him a portion with the great, and he shall divide the spoil with the strong; because he hath poured out his soul unto death: and he was numbered with the transgressors; and he bare the sin of many, and made intercession for the transgressors.* [226]

Here are a few more verses to illustrate what type of temple the Lord will build.

> *Matthew 16:13 When Jesus came into the coasts of Caesarea Philippi, he asked his disciples, saying, Whom do men say that I the Son of man am? 14 And they said, Some say that thou art John the Baptist: some, Elias; and others, Jeremias, or one of the prophets. 15 He saith unto them, But whom say ye that I am? 16 And Simon Peter answered and said, Thou art the Christ, the Son of the living God. 18b and upon this rock I will build my church; and the gates of hell shall not prevail against it.*[227]
>
> *Psalm 118:22 The stone which the builders refused is become the head stone of the corner.*
>
> *I Corinthians 3:11 For other foundation can no man lay than that is laid, which is Jesus Christ.*[228]
>
> *I Peter 2:5 Ye also, as lively stones, are built up a spiritual house, an holy priesthood, to offer up spiritual sacrifices, acceptable to God by Jesus Christ.*[229]

The temple the Lord will build is a spiritual temple, not a physical one.

I included all that explanation for one reason: the anointing of the most holy, just as with the rest of the purposes for the 70 Weeks, will be fulfilled on the day in which Jesus returns at the Second Coming. Much speculation exists regarding the Millennial Temple and how it will come to fruition. Will Jesus will build it? Will it be built for Him? Will He bring it with Him when He returns? Those questions become unnecessary if one puts the temple which will be built at the beginning of the 70th Week into play. Please allow me to explain.

In his article, Dr. Fruchtenbaum cited Ezekiel 40-48 as prooftext of a future time when the anointing of the most holy will occur. It regards the conclusion of Daniel's 70th Week. More specifically, the future fulfillment of the anointing of the most holy is contained in Ezekiel 43:1-5.

> *Ezekiel 43:1 Afterward he brought me to the gate, even the gate that looketh toward the east: 2 And, behold, the glory of the God of Israel came from the way of the east: and his voice was like a noise of many waters: and the earth shined with his glory. 3 And it was according to the appearance of the vision which I saw, even according to the vision that I saw when I came to destroy the city: and the visions were like the vision that I saw by the river Chebar; and I fell upon my face. 4 And the glory of the LORD came into the house by the way of the gate whose prospect is toward the east. 5 So the spirit took me up, and brought me into the inner court; and, behold, the glory of the LORD filled the house.*[230]

Ezekiel's vision, which encompasses the final 9 chapters of his book, regards the timing of the Second Coming, events which will occur on the day of the Second Coming, and some of the things which will occur within the Millennial Kingdom. I will discuss the timing aspect in Part Five of this study, but for the purposes of the anointing of the temple, I would be remiss if I did not point out the temple already exists when Jesus returns to anoint it.

Ezekiel 40-42 discusses, in very fine detail, the components of the Millennial Temple. When one compares those elements to Solomon's temple, one will see they are the same. Thus, the details we are given regarding Solomon's temple and the details we are given regarding Ezekiel's temple form a whole. Why do I point this out? Present rabbinical knowledge and assumptions aside, Ezekiel 43 provides us with one very important command the Jews will likely be reminded of prior to construction.

> *Ezekiel 43:10 <u>Thou son of man, shew the house to the house of Israel, that they may be ashamed of their iniquities: and let them measure the pattern. 11 And if they be ashamed of all that they have done, shew them the form of the house, and the fashion thereof, and the goings out thereof, and the comings in thereof, and all the forms thereof, and all the ordinances thereof, and all the forms thereof, and all the laws thereof: and write it in their sight, that they may keep the whole form thereof, and all the ordinances thereof, and do them.</u> 12 This is the law of the house; Upon the top of the mountain the whole limit thereof round about shall be most holy. Behold, this is the law of the house.*

When the second temple was built, the Jews were very aware it would not last. It was not built per the proper ordinances. However, there will come a time when a temple will be rebuilt, and it will be per the ordinances required of the everlasting dwelling of the Messiah. For this reason, it is difficult to conclude Zechariah 6 refers to the Lord building a physical temple when Ezekiel 43 regards Him dwelling forever in one built by instructions given to a sorrowful Israel intent on showing her God she is changed.

Therefore, it is my opinion much knowledge will likely be revealed to Israel prior to the rebuilding of this temple. Gog and Magog will change much for them. I cannot get more specific than that, because I do not have the details. However, Ezekiel 43 seems to shed light on how things will occur. Since we are not told the tribulation temple will be destroyed, we cannot assume it will be. And if it is not, it will be standing for the Lord to walk straight down from the Mount of Olives into on the day He returns, just as

He did on Palm Sunday in Matthew 21. Regardless, the anointing of the most holy will occur as stated in Ezekiel 43:1-5. Thus, the purposes for the 70 Weeks will be fulfilled.

Final Thoughts

It gives one an entirely different perspective regarding the events of the Day of the Lord when we consider only one day is in view. Furthermore, studying the purposes for the 70 Weeks and how they relate to Scripture seems to solidify this idea, at least in my opinion.

The Day of the Lord will begin with the Israel's cry for salvation after she comes to a saving knowledge of her Messiah. Jesus will return and save the tents of Judah first, which will be in Bozrah, before appearing in Jerusalem to judge the nations in the valley of decision. The armies which will have gathered at Megiddo in Revelation 16 will be making their way to Jerusalem to meet and defeat Jesus. This will not happen. Rather, the goats – those which have cursed Israel – will be laid waste. That includes the Antichrist and False Prophet. All the sheep – those which have blessed Israel – will be allowed entry into the Millennial Kingdom, along with Israel, herself. Israel will be brought into the New Covenant and will be the center of all Millennial Kingdom activity, including housing the throne of David whereupon Jesus will rule and reign for 1000 years.

PART FIVE: The Final Jubilee Year

An Overview of the End Times

We have now reached the capstone of this End Times Timeline study. In Part Five, we will look at the timing of the final jubilee year. Some who study the jubilees say we cannot know for sure when the final one will be, because Israel did not keep the jubilees for a significant number of years. I would counter such an assessment and posit that Israel's celebration of the jubilee years is insignificant in the scope of determining when the final jubilee year is. After all, God put the jubilee into place long ago. His timing is flawless and unchangeable, regardless of whether men do what they are supposed to. Thus, we should seek to use His determination of the jubilees, irrespective of whether they were kept.

As we make our way toward a determination of the final jubilee year, multiple data points will be used to establish a timeline of historical jubilees and other related Biblical events. We can then use history to determine the future, based on the way in which jubilees are counted. The overwhelming question then becomes - does the Bible give us enough information to calculate the final jubilee year?

My research into the final jubilee year began when I was referencing commentaries which explain the prophecy contained in Ezekiel 40:1. I have discussed at length how the chapters in Ezekiel are sequential, specifically regarding chapters 36-39. Ezekiel 36-37 regard Israel being gathered back into her land after having been away for almost 1900 years. After she comes to rest securely in her land and grows wealthy, a multitude of nations gathered by Gog will come against her for the purpose of taking a spoil. This plot is laid out in Ezekiel 38 and is what we refer to as The Battle of Gog and Magog. Further laid out in Ezekiel 38-39 is God's foiling of said plot and His absolute judgment of Gog and Gog's armies. God's overt actions will have an impact not only on Israel, but on the entirety of the world.

I have written at length about what I suspect the timing of this "battle" to be. I use quotation marks because it will not really wind up being a battle. God will have His way with the armies which come against Israel, purposing to bring Israel back to Him. One of the marks of the church age is that God does not act overtly. He also does not actively judge. Rather, He uses man to move along His prophetic plans. However, in Ezekiel 38-39, we see God shifting this paradigm. In five different verses in those two chapters, we are told God purposes to do two things: to make Himself known amongst the heathen nations and to elicit a specific response from Israel. God's actions through the Battle of Gog and Magog show us the church will have been already been removed.

Setting Gog and Magog aside, the last nine chapters in Ezekiel tell us of events which will occur at the Second Coming of Jesus Christ and at the beginning of His Millennial Kingdom. Therefore, we know the detailed battle in Ezekiel 38-39 will occur sometime after Israel is gathered back into her land (Ezekiel 36-37) and before the start of the Millennial Kingdom (Ezekiel 43-48). The crux of determining when those events may occur lies within the prophecy detailed in Ezekiel 40:1. There are two jubilee years in view in that one verse. However, before we look at Ezekiel 40:1 specifically, we need to make a distinction.

Restoration vs. Redemption

The easiest way to find the link between the Leviticus 25 concept of jubilee and its counterpart in the New Testament is to do a word study.

> *Leviticus 25:9 Then shalt thou cause the trumpet of the jubile to sound on the tenth day of the seventh month, in the day of atonement shall ye make the trumpet sound throughout all your land. 10 And ye shall hallow the fiftieth year, and proclaim liberty throughout all the land unto all the inhabitants thereof: it shall be a jubile unto you; and ye shall return every man unto his possession, and ye shall return every man unto his family.*

The proclamation of "liberty" refers to restoration. It not only allows for the return of rightful ownership, but it also denotes freedom from bondage. "Liberty" is the Hebrew word "derôr".[231] Its Greek counterpart is "aphesis". "Aphesis" means the following:

I. release from bondage or imprisonment
II. forgiveness or pardon, of sins (letting them go as if they had never been committed), remission of the penalty [232]

Below are two New Testament verses which show this concept of liberty, or "aphesis". It is the word "forgiveness".

> *Colossians 1:14 In whom we have redemption through his blood, even the forgiveness of sins:*[233]

> *Ephesians 1:7 In whom we have redemption through his blood, the forgiveness of sins, according to the riches of his grace;*[234]

219

We also see Jesus proclaiming "liberty" when He began to preach about the forgiveness of sin.

> *Luke 4:16 And he came to Nazareth, where he had been brought up: and, as his custom was, he went into the synagogue on the sabbath day, and stood up for to read. 17 And there was delivered unto him the book of the prophet Esaias. And when he had opened the book, he found the place where it was written, 18 The Spirit of the Lord is upon me, because he hath anointed me to preach the gospel to the poor; he hath sent me to heal the brokenhearted, to preach deliverance to the captives, and recovering of sight to the blind, to set at liberty them that are bruised, 19 To preach the acceptable year of the Lord. 20 And he closed the book, and he gave it again to the minister, and sat down. And the eyes of all them that were in the synagogue were fastened on him. 21 And he began to say unto them, This day is this scripture fulfilled in your ears.*[235]

You may have noticed striking similarities between Jesus's words in Luke 4 and the proclamation of liberty via the jubilee in Isaiah 61. We must note, however, Jesus was not proclaiming the jubilee "year". Rather, He was proclaiming the concept of jubilee, which is liberty via the forgiveness of sins and is consistent with Leviticus 25:9. This He came to do as "the Lamb of God, which taketh away the sins of the world" (John 1:29). In Luke's account, Jesus stopped quoting Isaiah 61 just before Isaiah wrote *"and the day of vengeance of our God;"* This is because the Second Coming and judgment of the unrighteous was not in view in Luke 4. Rather, liberty from the bondage of sin was being proclaimed via belief in Jesus Christ. For the church, liberty via the forgiveness of sins is forward-looking to the day of "redemption", not the day of "restoration".

> *Revelation 5:9 And they sung a new song, saying, Thou art worthy to take the book, and to open the seals thereof: for thou wast slain, and hast redeemed us to God by thy blood out of every kindred, and tongue, and people, and nation;*[236]

The word "redeemed" in the above text is the Greek word "agorazó".[237] "Agorazó" means the following:

> 59 */agorázō* ("acquire by purchasing") stresses *transfer* – i.e. where something becomes *another's belonging* (*possession*). In salvation-contexts, 59 (*agorázō*) is *not* redeeming ("buying back"), but rather focuses on how the believer now *belongs to the Lord as His unique possession* (J. Thayer). Indeed, Christ purchases all the privileges and responsibilities that go with *belonging to Him* (being *in Christ*).

I underlined a portion of the text above to underscore the difference between the concept of redemption and the concept of restoration. Restoration means someone owned or possessed something, went for a time without possession, then received possession back. However, redemption is a one-time transfer of ownership whereupon all rights permanently pass from seller to buyer.

> *II Corinthians 5:17 Therefore if any man be in Christ, he is a new creature: old things are passed away; behold, all things are become new.*[238]

When we accept Jesus Christ as our Savior, our debts are immediately forgiven. We are then sealed by the Holy Spirit for the day of redemption.

> *Ephesians 4:30 And grieve not the holy Spirit of God, whereby ye are sealed unto the day of redemption.*[239]

> *Ephesians 1:13 In whom ye also trusted, after that ye heard the word of truth, the gospel of your salvation: in whom also after that ye believed, ye were sealed with that holy Spirit of promise, 14 Which is the earnest of our inheritance until the redemption of the purchased possession, unto the praise of his glory.*[240]

> *Romans 8:23 And not only they, but ourselves also, which have the firstfruits of the Spirit, even we ourselves groan within ourselves, waiting for the adoption, to wit, the redemption of our body.*[241]

The day of our redemption is the rapture of the church. That the rapture of the church, or the day of redemption, will have already occurred was noted in Revelation 5:9 where the elders are seen singing about having been redeemed. That the rapture, or the day of redemption, will be pre-tribulation or pre-70th Week was inferred in Revelation 5:9 where the elders are seen singing about having been redeemed while Jesus is seen holding the yet unopened seven-sealed scroll.

The concept of redemption vs. restoration is also captured in Romans 11.

> *Romans 11:17 And if some of the branches be broken off, and thou, being a wild olive tree, wert grafted in among them, and with them partakest of the root and fatness of the olive tree;*

> *21 For if God spared not the natural branches, take heed lest he also spare not thee. 22 Behold therefore the goodness and severity of God: on them which fell, severity; but toward thee, goodness, if thou continue in his goodness: otherwise thou also shalt be cut off. 23 And they also, if they abide not*

> *still in unbelief, shall be grafted in: for God is able to graft them in again.*[242]

The natural branches, which represent Israel, were broken off and will be grafted back in. That speaks of restoration. However, the wild olive tree, which represents the church, is grafted in only once. That speaks of redemption and the one-time transaction. An article written by Chuck Missler on www.khouse.org supports this idea.

> *"When property is sold in our culture, title is usually passed in fee simple, in perpetuity to the buyer. However, Israels land was granted, in the days of Joshua, to the tribes to be retained within the family. (Thats one of the reasons genealogies were so important.)*
>
> *When someone sold a property" to pay debts, or whatever" the transaction was what we would view as a lease: there were provisions for the land to eventually return to the family. A title deed included the terms that a kinsman of the family could perform to redeem the property to the family."*[243]

At the end of the 70th Week, and at the Second Coming of Jesus Christ, Israel will be delivered from her enemies. Salvation will be granted to her via the New Covenant, and rightful ownership of her land and possessions will be restored. She will finally have her place atop the nations in the Kingdom. Conversely, the church will have been redeemed seven years prior.

The concept of liberty being proclaimed via the forgiveness of sins is a sort of jubilee. This jubilee corresponds to the entire church age, during which the forgiveness of sins is available to anyone who believes in Jesus Christ. However, the church is a largely Gentile group. The specific jubilee year regards Israel. Having said all that, we will now look at the prophecy in Ezekiel 40:1.

The Prophecy in Ezekiel 40:1

The prophecy given in Ezekiel 40:1 is the foundation for this entire study. Without Ezekiel pinpointing exact years, it would be nearly impossible to surmise where to begin counting from. It should be understood there are difficulties in pinning down specific years and their corresponding events due to the number of sources available which support conflicting information. However, I will do my best to support the positions I take and fully explain how I arrived at my conclusions. Let us begin by looking at Ezekiel 40:1.

> *Ezekiel 40:1 In the five and twentieth year of our captivity, in the beginning of the year, in the tenth day of the month, in the fourteenth year after that the city was smitten, in the selfsame day the hand of the LORD was upon me, and brought me thither.*[244]

Ezekiel's vision occurred in the beginning of the year, on the tenth day of the month. As we have learned previously, the sabbatical years and cycles were established on that same day, Nisan 10. Joshua 4 taught us this. Therefore, Ezekiel was given this vision on the first day of a new sabbatical year. As we develop the timeline, it will become apparent the year of Ezekiel's vision also had other significance. We will be able to identify Ezekiel's vision not only occurred on the first day of a new sabbatical year. We will also be able to identify Ezekiel's vision occurred on the first day of a jubilee year.

To begin the jubilee timeline, we need to ascertain which year Ezekiel was in when he received his vision. Two clues are given to aid us in this determination. We are told the specific year was the 25th year of "our captivity" and 14 years after "the city was smitten".

The Captivity and the Destruction of the City and Temple

There were three different exiles which occurred during the whole of the Babylonian Captivity. We are looking for the specific year in which one of those three exiles occurred, as well as for the year in which the city was destroyed. We will start with the year the city was destroyed which happens to be the same year Solomon's temple was destroyed.

    There are two primary fields of thought regarding the timing of this event. Most sources place the destruction of the city and Solomon's temple in 586 B.C. Other sources place the destructions in 587 B.C. There are various other thoughts out there, but determining this timeline is not as simple as isolating one date. There are several reference points which must align perfectly, or else the timeline cannot be accurate. Each of the other data points will be explained in greater detail as we move along with our research.

    For the calculation of this timeline, the year I used for the destruction of the city and Solomon's temple was neither 586 nor 587 B.C. The year I chose to use was obtained from a few different sources. I say "a few" because I did not continue looking beyond being able to validate the claim in three places. I will provide more comprehensive details in just a bit, but the year was validated by the research of Bishop James Ussher and backed up by <u>Answers in Genesis</u>.

    For the sake of data integrity and having come to understand the fallacy that is Tishri 10-Tishri 10 respective to jubilee years, I am excluding the third source I used during my initial research. I will use only Ussher's research for the construction of this timeline. However, before we get to those sources, we need to understand more about the timeline of the Babylonian Captivity since it was within the Captivity the destruction of the Solomon's temple occurred.

The most common dates for the start of the Babylonian Captivity are 606 B.C. and 605 B.C. Obviously if the start dates are different, the year to which Ezekiel's prophecy applies, as well as the year in which the city and temple were destroyed, would also be different. When calculating the dates for the Captivity, there are three Judaic kings involved: Jehoiakim, Jehoiachin, and Zedekiah. We are given the lengths of their reigns: 11 years, 3 months, and 11 years, respectively. Furthermore, we are told in two different passages of Scripture during which year of Jehoiakim's reign the first exile occurred.

> *Jeremiah 46:1 The word of the LORD which came to Jeremiah the prophet against the Gentiles; 2 Against Egypt, against the army of Pharaohnecho king of Egypt, which was by the river Euphrates in Carchemish, which Nebuchadrezzar king of Babylon smote in the fourth year of Jehoiakim the son of Josiah king of Judah.*[245]

Compare this to Daniel 1:1, which says:

> *Daniel 1:1 In the third year of the reign of Jehoiakim king of Judah came Nebuchadnezzar king of Babylon unto Jerusalem, and besieged it.*[246]

The first logical question would be – did this exile occur in the fourth year of Jehoiakim's reign or in the third year? The verses seem to be at odds with one another, but they are not. Jeremiah, living in the land of Israel, was using a Hebraic method of determining dates based on the Hebrew calendar. Daniel, already living in Babylon, would have been using a Babylonian system. Therefore, they would have been working from different starting points. Even a matter of a few months can make a big difference.

So where does that leave us?

> *"First of all the exact date is 607 BC according to Bishop Ussher, not 606 BC. This was indeed the first year of the reign of Nebuchadnezzar if we just count as the Bible counts. And the first year of Jehoiakim starts in 610 BC. As our years don't fit nicely into the reigns of the kings (different starting month), the third year is 607 BC."*[247]

I mentioned three sources which I used to develop my timeline. The first was Bishop James Ussher. For those of you who may be unfamiliar with him, here is a bit about Bishop Ussher.

> *"James Ussher (or Usher; 4 January 1581 – 21 March 1656) was the Irish Archbishop of Armagh and Primate of All Ireland between 1625 and 1656. He was a prolific scholar and church leader, who today is most famous for his chronology that sought to establish the time and date of the creation...*
>
> *Ussher's work was a project supporting Young Earth Creationism, which holds that the universe was created, not billions of years ago, but thousands. But while calculating the date of the Creation is today considered a controversial activity, in Ussher's time such a calculation was still regarded as an important task, one previously attempted by many Post-Reformation scholars, such as Joseph Justus Scaliger and physicist Isaac Newton."*[248]

Below is Ussher's chronology of the events which led to the destruction of the Solomon's temple:

Ussher's Chronology:

610: Jehoiakim is made king by Pharaoh Nechoh, see 2 Kg. 23:34.
608: Nebuchadnezzar is made viceroy.
607: battle of Carchemish, where Egypt was defeated (fourth year of Jehoiakim), see Jer. 46:2.
607: first siege of Jerusalem by Nebuchadnezzar; Daniel and his friends taken and brought to Babylon, start of the 70 years of captivity.
605: death of Nabopolassar, father of Nebuchadnezzar.
604: Jehoiakim rebels (2 Kg. 24:1), it takes Nebuchadnezzar a few years to be able to respond.
600: Nebuchadnezzar invades Judah, see 2 Kg. 24:2.
599: second siege of Jerusalem; Jehoiakim's son Jeconiah, also Jehoiachin, was taken to Babylon (Jer. 27:20), see also 2 Kg. 24:12.
589: last siege of Jerusalem by Nebuchadnezzar.
588: destruction of the first temple.

"Note that secular history gives 586 BC as the date that Solomon's temple was destroyed. And note that Bishop Ussher's starts the reign of Nebuchadnezzar two years earlier than secular history."[249]

The following is what <u>Answers in Genesis</u> had to say regarding Ussher's work:

Answers in Genesis:

The response given about Ussher's calculation of dates regarded his determination of the year of creation. Even so, the information remains applicable in this case.

"Ussher started from the Bible and not from secular history. That is why he used a date of 588 BC for the fall of Jerusalem and not 586 BC. He noted that the fourth year of King Jehoiakim's reign corresponded to the first year of Nebuchadnezzar's reign. (Jeremiah 25:1) In working through the king lists of Judah, he determined that this was in 607 BC, two years before the death of Nebuchadnezzar's father. His father died in 605 BC and many historians concluded that this was the start of Nebuchadnezzar's reign when in fact he was already ruling as viceroy for two years. It was the normal procedure to count as the first year of the reign of a king from the year he became a viceroy. Starting from the Bible, Ussher was able to correct this error in secular history.

So was Ussher Right?

Ussher was neither charlatan nor naive; in fact, he was one of the most learned men of his day. Understanding the assumptions with which he began his calculations (particularly the one we should all begin with, namely that God's Word is true and reliable), we can readily understand how he arrived at his date for creation. In fact, if one assumes that there are no deliberate 'jumps' or gaps in the later genealogies (for which the evidence in my view is inadequate), then his date is a perfectly reasonable deduction based on his detailed knowledge of and reverence for the Word of God."[250]

These sources suggest the destruction of Solomon's temple occurred in 588 B.C, or in Hebrew year 588-87 on a Nisan-Nisan calendar. This timeline works with scripture and with the timeline of the Judaic kings. Let us look at Ezekiel 40:1 again to remind us what other information we are searching for.

> *Ezekiel 40:1 In the five and twentieth year of our captivity, in the beginning of the year, in the tenth day of the month, in the fourteenth year after that the city was smitten, in the selfsame day the hand of the LORD was upon me, and brought me thither.*

We are looking for the 25th year of captivity, which was also 14 years after the city was smitten. The year in which the city was smitten is the same year in which the temple was destroyed: 588 B.C., according to Ussher. There were, however, three different exiles during the Babylonian Captivity. If 588 B.C. is the correct year the city was smitten, 14 years later would be 575 B.C. Remember, we must count the remainder of the existing year as "year one". Thus, we would expect to see an exile around 599 B.C. to know we are on the right track.

Indeed, from the source above, we do find that very thing. The second exile of the Babylonian Captivity occurred in 599 B.C. Thus, we have identified the potential year for Ezekiel's prophecy as 575 B.C., which would have also been a jubilee year.

Below is a chart of everything I just went over regarding the Babylonian Captivity, the chronology of the Judaic kings, and the destruction of the first temple.

The 70 Years of the Babylonian Captivity

610	600	590	580	570	560	550	540
609	599	589	579	569	559	549	539
608	598	588	578	568	558	548	538
607	597	587	577	567	557	547	
606	596	586	576	566	556	546	
605	595	585	575	565	555	545	
604	594	584	574	564	554	544	
603	593	583	573	563	553	543	
602	592	582	572	562	552	542	
601	591	581	571	561	551	541	

Battle of Carchemish - First Babylonian Captivity (Jeremiah 46:2/Daniel 1:1)
Jehoiakim's reign - 11 years (II Kings 23:36) Nisan 610 - Shevat 600 BC
Jehoiachin's reign - 3 months - Kislev 600 - Adar 600 BC (II Kings 24:8)
Second Babylonian Exile - Nisan 599 BC
Zedekiah's Reign (II Kings 25:2) - Nisan 599 BC - 588 BC/Destruction of Temple
End of Zedekiah's Reign/Sacking of Jerusalem/Desruction of First Temple (II Kings 2:8)
Ezekiel 40:1's 14-year count (also after 25 years in captivity starting from the Second Exile in
In the 25th Year of Captivity (Ezekiel 40:1)
Ezekiel's vision in a Jubilee Year of a Future Jubilee Year
End of Babylonian Captivity (607-538)

Entering the Promised Land

The immediate inclination after arriving at this date might be to jump forward and figure out where we are regarding the final jubilee year. However, before we can proceed forward, we must first go backward to establish whether the jubilee year determined above – 575 B.C. – fits in with the timing of the exodus from Egypt and with the Israelites entering their Promised Land. If it does not fit, since entry into the Promised Land was the first jubilee established, we will have a problem.

A jubilee, as calculated per Leviticus 25, is the start of the 50th year after a cycle of 7-7s, or 49 years. The dates below are calculated backward from the jubilee year we just established: 575 B.C. As you can see, this dates the entrance of the Israelites into their Promised Land in the spring of 1408 B.C.

Jubilees Since Entry into Promised Land until...? (70)								
1408	918							
1359	869							
1310	820							
1261	771							
1212	722							
1163	673							
1114	624							
1065	575							
1016								
967								

The more common date typically referred to regarding the whole of the exodus is not the date the Israelites entered their land. Rather, it is usually the date of their exodus from Egypt. Fortunately, I put a chart together to calculate those years so we can see if we are still on the right track. I will get to that in just a moment.

First, we need to know when the Israelites entered the wilderness. Secondly, we need to know how long they were there. Finally, we need to know when they exited the wilderness and entered their land.

> *Exodus 16:1 And they took their journey from Elim, and all the congregation of the children of Israel came unto the wilderness of Sin, which is between Elim and Sinai, on the fifteenth day of the second month after their departing out of the land of Egypt. ² And the whole congregation of the children of Israel murmured against Moses and Aaron in the wilderness: ³ And the children of Israel said unto them, Would to God we had died by the hand of the LORD in the land of Egypt, when we sat by the flesh pots, and when we did eat bread to the full; for ye have brought us forth into this wilderness, to kill this whole assembly with hunger.*
> *⁴ Then said the LORD unto Moses, Behold, I will rain bread from heaven for you; and the people shall go out and gather a certain rate every day, that I may prove them, whether they will walk in my law, or no.*[251]

The Israelites entered the wilderness on Iyyar 15, exactly 30 days after having left Egypt. At that time, the Lord began providing them with manna. How long did their provisions last?

> *Exodus 16:35 And the children of Israel did eat manna forty years, until they came to a land inhabited; they did eat manna, until they came unto the borders of the land of Canaan.*[252]

The Israelites ate manna for 40 years, until they entered their land. To ensure a correct count of years, we need to know when the Israelites stopped eating manna.

> *Deuteronomy 1:3 And it came to pass in the fortieth year, in the eleventh month, on the first day of the month, that Moses spake unto the children of Israel, according unto all that the LORD had given him in commandment unto them; 4 After he*

had slain Sihon the king of the Amorites, which dwelt in Heshbon, and Og the king of Bashan, which dwelt at Astaroth in Edrei: 5 On this side Jordan, in the land of Moab, began Moses to declare this law, saying, 6 The LORD our God spake unto us in Horeb, saying, Ye have dwelt long enough in this mount: 7 Turn you, and take your journey, and go to the mount of the Amorites, and unto all the places nigh thereunto, in the plain, in the hills, and in the vale, and in the south, and by the sea side, to the land of the Canaanites, and unto Lebanon, unto the great river, the river Euphrates. 8 Behold, I have set the land before you: go in and possess the land which the LORD sware unto your fathers, Abraham, Isaac, and Jacob, to give unto them and to their seed after them.[253]

Joshua 5:10 And the children of Israel encamped in Gilgal, and kept the passover on the fourteenth day of the month at even in the plains of Jericho. 11 And they did eat of the old corn of the land on the morrow after the passover, unleavened cakes, and parched corn in the selfsame day. 12 And the manna ceased on the morrow after they had eaten of the old corn of the land; neither had the children of Israel manna any more; but they did eat of the fruit of the land of Canaan that year.[254]

Based on the text from Deuteronomy 1, a full 40 years must be counted. Our years run from Nisan 10-Nisan 10, and because the Israelites did not stop eating manna until Nisan 15, we must count 5 days into the 41st year. The commentary below might explain things a bit more clearly.

"The children of Israel did eat manna forty years. Kalisch observes that the actual time was not forty full years, but about one month short of that period, since the manna began after the fifteenth day of the second month of the first

*year (verse 1) and terminated just after Passover of the **forty-first year** (Joshua 5:10-12).*"[255]

In the previous chart, counting jubilees backward from 575 B.C. would place the jubilee year which saw Israel entering her Promised Land in 1408 B.C.

Exodus 1448 BC - Spring/40 Years in Wilderness to Spring/Entry into Promised Land				
1448	1438	1428	1418	**1408**
1447	1437	1427	1417	
1446	1436	1426	1416	
1445	1435	1425	1415	
1444	1434	1424	1414	
1443	1433	1423	1413	
1442	1432	1422	1412	
1441	1431	1421	1411	
1440	1430	1420	1410	
1439	1429	1419	1409	

This chart calculates 40 full years in the wilderness, accounting for the 5 days from the start of the 41st year until the Feast of Unleavened Bread, which was the end of the Lord's provisions of manna. Thus, we have a spring-to-spring count of the 39 years and 11 months the Israelites ate manna. Our spring-to-spring dates run from Iyyar 15 in 1448 B.C. to Nisan 15 in 1408 B.C.

The next logical question would be:

Did the Israelites' exodus from Egypt occur in 1448 B.C.?

To answer that question more accurately, we need to jump a few hundred years ahead and look at some specific information pertaining to King Solomon.

The Reign of King Solomon

Establishing the year of the exodus requires calculating dates for the reign of Solomon and the construction of his temple. Let us begin by looking at a key verse in I Kings 6 which will help us to further add to our jubilee timeline.

> *I Kings 6:1 And it came to pass in the four hundred and eightieth year after the children of Israel were come out of the land of Egypt, in the fourth year of Solomon's reign over Israel, in the month Zif, which is the second month, that he began to build the house of the LORD.*[256]

Like the calculations required by Ezekiel 40:1, we also have calculations required by I Kings 6:1 to help us pinpoint another specific year. In Ezekiel 40:1, we had to identify the specific year which was 25 years after one of the three exiles and 14 years after the city was smitten. In I Kings 6:1, we must identify a year which was the 480th year after the exodus, which was also the fourth year of Solomon's reign. Since we are attempting to determine if 1448 B.C. is the year of the exodus, we must then calculate the years of Solomon's reign to determine if we are on the right track. If we are, the years in view in I Kings 6:1 will lead us to 1448 B.C.

As with most of these ancient dates, there is no consensus. However, most of the sources available place Solomon's reign sometime between 971 and 930 B.C. II Chronicles 9 tells us exactly how long Solomon reigned.

> *II Chronicles 9:30 And Solomon reigned in Jerusalem over all Israel forty years. 31 And Solomon slept with his fathers, and he was buried in the city of David his father: and Rehoboam his son reigned in his stead.*[257]

One of the biggest impediments to determining the correct span of years for Solomon's reign is the issue of whether Judaic kings started reigning in the month of Nisan or the month of Tishri. Rabbinical Judaism states the kings began reigning in the month of Tishri, which is in the fall. However, I Kings 6:1 infers the reign of the Judaic kings began in the month of Nisan, which is in the spring. The following excerpts, taken from an article written by Bible prophecy scholar Gary Stearman, will help us clear this up.

> *"Although the fall festival of Rosh HaShanah marks the first day of the new Jewish calendar year, Nisan in the spring is actually considered the beginning of the annual festival cycle. The Jewish commentaries in the Mishnah tell us that the year of the reign of Jewish kings was counted from Nisan in biblical times.*
>
> *In fact, in the traditional Jewish calendar, there are four legal New Year's days: First comes Nisan, the New Year for Kings.*
>
> *As we shall see, recognition of the first New Year celebration in the Jewish calendar becomes extremely important in understanding the finished work of Christ. When He came to His people two thousand years ago, He completed every tiny detail of prophecy. In particular, His coronation as King was no mere metaphor; it was perfect and complete.*
>
> *Christians remember how our Deliverer, Christ, the Lamb of God, was sacrificed for us. We recall His public humiliation, His death and His resurrection. He was given a thorny crown on that day. It was painful and demeaning, but it was a real and legitimate crown, representing an actual coronation.*

New Year for Kings

Before we revisit the events of His last Passover, we should review a little-known but interesting fact about this day, traditionally remembered by the Jews as the day when the kings of ancient Israel were crowned.

In fact, Nisan – the month of the Passover – marked what was known as the "New Year for Kings."

One essay on the subject says,

"For reasons as yet unclear, the beginning of the year, reckoned from the spring by the early postexilic community, came to be celebrated in the autumn in Judaism. The sounding of the ram's horn (shofar) figured prominently in the ritual of the festival, held on Tishri 1-2, while the liturgy emphasized the themes of judgment, God's kingship, and creation.

"Nisan 1 continued to be recognized as New Year's day for the reckoning of the reigns of Jewish kings and for festivals. Thus, although the calendar year began with Tishri 1, Passover was regarded as the first festival of the year. Of minor significance were the New Year's days on Elul 1 and Shevat 1, for the tithing of cattle and for trees respectively." [Old Testament Essays 1967-1998, Vol. 1, Sheffield Academic Press, 1998]

Israel's two diasporas – in 722 and 586 B.C. – and the collapse of the Jewish Monarchy led to the recognition of Tishri and Rosh HaShanah, rather than Nisan and Passover, as the head of the year. Put another way, Jews came to honor the Civil New Year in the fall, rather than the Spiritual New Year in the spring.

The following quote from The Jewish Voice further clarifies this view:

"How do we know that Passover is Rosh HaShanah for the Kings? It is in the Tanach [Old Testament], though somewhat hidden. How do we know that the Kings of Israel are crowned at Passover? In I Kings, it says this: '... in the fourth year of Solomon's reign over Israel, in the month of Zif, which is the second month, that he began to build the House of Adonai.' (I Kings 6:1) It is repeated in II Chronicles 3:2 as well. The second month of the reign of King Solomon – which means Solomon was crowned the month before! The month of Zif is now known as the month of Iyar, which comes after the month of Nisan, when Passover is. From this understanding, we can check it with the other kings of Israel as well. There was a debate between the House of Hillel and the House of Shamai, whether it was on the 15th or the 1st of the month, but the 15th is Passover night, and this became the common understanding."

In the ancient world, then, Israelites regarded the 1st of Nisan as the New Year for Kings, and the festival of Passover as the actual coronation day.

Little known to Gentiles, this amazing truth throws new light on that most historic of all Passovers. The day that Jesus was crucified was also the traditional Jewish day for the Coronation of Kings!

The Coronation

On the morning of that day – Passover, the 15th of Nisan – Jesus was given a public coronation, recognized by both

Roman and Jewish leaders. As we shall see, this fact is carefully documented in Scripture.

And thus, in Nisan, the month of the New Year for Kings, and on Passover the Day of Coronation, Jesus was recognized by both Jewish and Gentile leaders as the King. Furthermore, He had been enrobed, crowned and formally presented. Everything required for a legitimate coronation had been accomplished. And ever since that eminent day, Scripture has stood as its witness."[258]

We learned in II Chronicles 9:30 that Solomon reigned for a full 40 years. Because his coronation would have occurred in the spring, we need to use the same spring-to-spring method of calculating the years as we have for everything else. There are two more popular dates for both the start of his reign (971 B.C. and 970 B.C.) and the end of his reign (931 B.C. and 930 B.C.). Because we began this timeline with a less popular date, neither of those date ranges for Solomon's reign will work. Rather, a range of 972-32 would have to be used to lead us to back to 1448. Read on to see how this is the case.

Solomon's 40 Year Reign - Passover to Passover				
972	962	952	942	932
971	961	951	941	
970	960	950	940	
969	959	949	939	
968	958	948	938	
967	957	947	937	
966	956	946	936	
965	955	945	935	
964	954	944	934	
963	953	943	933	

As with the calculation of the extra days in the 41st year of eating manna in the wilderness, the 4 days from Nisan 10 – Nisan 14 would need to be counted in the 41st year to accomplish an entire 40-year reign. Thus, if we use these dates, Solomon's reign would have lasted from the spring of 972 B.C. to the spring of 932 B.C.

The second piece of information we are given in I Kings 6:1 to calculate our specific year is that temple construction began in the second month of the fourth year of Solomon's reign. If the chart above is accurate, that year would be 969 B.C. I Kings 6:1 further tells us the fourth year of Solomon' reign was the 480th year after the Israelites came out of Egypt. Below is a chart showing the calculation of 480 years, keeping with the spring-to-spring dates.

	1-10	11-20	21-30	31-40	41-50	51-60	61-70	71-80	+ 400
	969	979	989	999	1009	1019	1029	1039	1439
	970	980	990	1000	1010	1020	1030	1040	1440
	971	981	991	1001	1011	1021	1031	1041	1441
Counting	972	982	992	1002	1012	1022	1032	1042	1442
Back to the	973	983	993	1003	1013	1023	1033	1043	1443
Exodus	974	984	994	1004	1014	1024	1034	1044	1444
	975	985	995	1005	1015	1025	1035	1045	1445
	976	986	996	1006	1016	1026	1036	1046	1446
	977	987	997	1007	1017	1027	1037	1047	1447
	978	988	998	1008	1018	1028	1038	1048	1448

Let us revisit I Kings 6:1 to look at the specific text of the verse.

> *I Kings 6:1 And it came to pass in the four hundred and eightieth year after the children of Israel were come out of the land of Egypt, in the fourth year of Solomon's reign over Israel, in the month Zif, which is the second month, that he began to build the house of the LORD.*[259]

Counting 480 years backward from the 4th year of Solomon's reign, assuming a starting year of 972 B.C., we arrive at the year of the Israelites' exodus from Egypt: 1448 B.C. Because we know Solomon reigned a full 40 years, we cannot place the dates of his reign from 970-931 B.C. We would not have enough years. If we place the dates of Solomon's reign from 971-930 B.C., we would have too many years. If we place the dates from 970-930 B.C., we wind up with an entirely different jubilee timeline. Shifting the years of Solomon's reign would necessitate using different years for the rest of the data points in question: the exodus from Egypt, the Israelites' entry into their Promised Land, the reigns of the Judaic kings, the exiles in Babylon, the destruction of Solomon's temple, and the year of Ezekiel's vision. The years which have been calculated thus far appear as such:

972 B.C., 932 B.C., 969 B.C., 1408 B.C., 1448 B.C., 599 B.C., 588 B.C., and 575 B.C.

A shift in one year would necessitate a shift in all the years, and we would have to determine whether there is sufficient evidence with which to do so. Our timeline would then appear as follows:

971 B.C., 931 B.C., 968 B.C., 1407 B.C., 1447 B.C., 598 B.C., 587 B.C, and 574 B.C.

And if we wanted to take it a step further and use a third set of data points which are perhaps just as popular, if not more so, we could use the following data set:

970 B.C., 930 B.C., 967 B.C., 1406 B.C., 1446 B.C., 597 B.C., 586 B.C, and 573 B.C.

There is reputable sourcing, and perhaps even more popular sourcing, to substantiate each of the last two data sets. The biggest difference with some of this sourcing lies within the use of fall dates to calculate corresponding years and events rather than the use of spring dates. This is potentially problematic because it places events in different Hebrew years when using fall-to-fall calculations. However, it is not outside the realm of possibility that the second or third sets of data are accurate. The hardship of knowing which data set to use stems from the wealth of information available and deciding which sources are accurate. This does not make the calculation of the final jubilee year impossible. It only gives us several potential years to look at. However, only one is correct.

For the time being, let us move along with our research.

The Exodus from Egypt

I posed a question before I presented the research regarding Solomon.

Did the Israelites' exodus from Egypt occur in 1448 B.C.?

The most popular date for the exodus is 1446 B.C. which was shown in the tertiary timeline. A secondary possibility exists where 1447 might be the correct year. For brevity's sake, and because the rest of the data has already been discussed at length, we will simply say 1448 "could be" accurate. It also may not be. However, it is now time to move forward in our jubilee timeline instead of backwards. Let us take another look at the jubilee timeline.

The Jubilee Years from B.C. to A.D.

Since we have now substantiated the jubilee timeline as begun with the dates of Ezekiel's vision and the Israelites' entry into the Promised Land, we can now start filling in the rest of the jubilee chart. Please be mindful of the fact that the continued timeline uses the data set from data set one, not two or three. Both of those other data sets will be shown in a bit.

Jubilees Since Entry into Promised Land until...? (70)							
1408	918	428					
1359	869	379					
1310	820	330					
1261	771	281					
1212	722	232					
1163	673	183					
1114	624	134					
1065	575	85					
1016	526	36					
967	477	14					

The boxes in orange denote the shift from B.C. to A.D. For you to see the count and not just take my word for how I arrived at these jubilee years, I have included another chart below showing 14 A.D. is, indeed, the start of the 50th year from 36 B.C. This accounts for no year "0".

	These years denote the switch from B.C. to A.D. Please see the validation below to show there are, indeed, 49 years between the two date cells above.							
1	**36**	29	22	15	8	1BC-1AD	7	**14**
2	35	28	21	14	7	1	8	
3	34	27	20	13	6	2	9	
4	33	26	19	12	5	3	10	
5	32	25	18	11	4	4	11	
6	31	24	17	10	3	5	12	
7	30	23	16	9	2	6	13	

The next step to find the "final" jubilee year is to simply bring the same count forward.

The Final Jubilee Year – Revealed

According to the first data set used, the "final" jubilee year will begin on Nisan 10 in our year of 2023. Below are restatements of the data points used in the calculation of each timeline. But before anyone gets too crazy, we still have to talk about what event is prophesied to occur at the beginning of the "final" jubilee year. There is much left to discuss. For now, the restatements of the data points are below.

Data Set One:

Jubilees Since Entry into Promised Land until...? (70)

1408	918	428	63	553	1043	1533	2023
1359	869	379	112	602	1092	1582	
1310	820	330	161	651	1141	1631	
1261	771	281	210	700	1190	1680	
1212	722	232	259	749	1239	1729	
1163	673	183	308	798	1288	1778	
1114	624	134	357	847	1337	1827	
1065	575	85	406	896	1386	1876	
1016	526	36	455	945	1435	1925	
967	477	14	504	994	1484	1974	

Solomon's Reign: 972-932 B.C.
Beginning of Construction of Solomon's Temple: 969 B.C.
Second Exile of the Babylonian Captivity: 599 B.C.
Destruction of Jerusalem and Solomon's Temple: 588 B.C.
Exodus from Egypt: 1448 B.C.
Entry into the Promised Land: 1408 B.C.
Ezekiel's Vision: 575 B.C.

Data Set Two:

Jubilees Since Entry into Promised Land until...? (70)

1407	917	427	64	554	1044	1534	2024
1358	868	378	113	603	1093	1583	
1309	819	329	162	652	1142	1632	
1260	770	280	211	701	1191	1681	
1211	721	231	260	750	1240	1730	
1162	672	182	309	799	1289	1779	
1113	623	133	358	848	1338	1828	
1064	574	84	407	897	1387	1877	
1015	525	35	456	946	1436	1926	
966	476	15	505	995	1485	1975	

Solomon's Reign: 971-931 B.C.
Beginning of Construction of Solomon's Temple: 968 B.C.
Second Exile of the Babylonian Captivity: 598 B.C.
Destruction of Jerusalem and Solomon's Temple: 587 B.C.
Exodus from Egypt: 1447 B.C.
Entry into the Promised Land: 1407 B.C.
Ezekiel's Vision: 574 B.C.

Data Set Three:

Jubilees Since Entry into Promised Land until....? (70)

1406	916	426	65	555	1045	1535		2025
1357	867	377	114	604	1094	1584		
1308	818	328	163	653	1143	1633		
1259	769	279	212	702	1192	1682		
1210	720	230	261	751	1241	1731		
1161	671	181	310	800	1290	1780		
1112	622	132	359	849	1339	1829		
1063	573	83	408	898	1388	1878		
1014	524	34	457	947	1437	1927		
965	475	16	506	996	1486	1976		

Solomon's Reign: 970-930 B.C.
Beginning of Construction of Solomon's Temple: 967 B.C.
Second Exile of the Babylonian Captivity: 597 B.C.
Destruction of Jerusalem and Solomon's Temple: 586 B.C.
Exodus from Egypt: 1446 B.C.
Entry into the Promised Land: 1406 B.C.
Ezekiel's Vision: 573 B.C.

Final Thoughts

This book contains updated jubilee research. If you wish to learn more about the "final" jubilee year, please read my latest book entitled *The Jubilee and Ezekiel's Temple*.

I don't believe there is much left to say at this point. I hope all the research speaks for itself. Thus, I will simply leave you with my final thoughts. They really aren't even my thoughts, but words spoken by our King of Kings and Lord of Lords.

> *Matthew 28:18 And Jesus came and spake unto them, saying, All power is given unto me in heaven and in earth. 19 Go ye therefore, and teach all nations, baptizing them in the name of the Father, and of the Son, and of the Holy Ghost: 20 Teaching them to observe all things whatsoever I have commanded you: and, lo, I am with you always, even unto the end of the world. Amen.*[260]

Because the rapture of the church precedes all the events outlined in Parts 1-5 of this End Times Timeline, it is incumbent upon us to make the most of every day we remain here. Time is very short, my friends. Let us all do everything we can to spread the gospel of Jesus Christ.

Thank you for taking this journey with me. I hope, if nothing else, you learned a few things. May God bless you all.

Coming Soon!!

The Judgment of the Summer Fruit

A Follow-up to the End Times Timeline

Available in January 2017!

About the Author

Heather lives in Michigan with her son and her cat. She has a Master's degree in Management from Walsh College and is currently employed as an analyst. When not working, she can usually be found at home researching Bible prophecy or with her nose stuck in a book. Heather has a YouTube channel which she uses to teach Bible prophecy. She also conducts routine Bible studies using the "chapter-by-chapter, verse-by verse" methodology. Her YouTube channel is named "Heather R", and she hopes you will stop by and visit sometime.

This is Heather's first self-published work.

References

[1] https://www.biblegateway.com/passage/?search=proverbs+25%3A2&version=KJV
[2] https://www.biblegateway.com/passage/?search=daniel+9%3A24-27&version=KJV
[3] http://www.khouse.org/enews_article/2007/1190/print/
[4] https://www.biblegateway.com/passage/?search=matthew+21&version=KJV
[5] https://www.biblegateway.com/passage/?search=titus+2%3A13-14&version=KJV
[6] https://www.biblegateway.com/passage/?search=matthew+24%3A32-34&version=KJV
[7] https://www.biblegateway.com/passage/?search=ezekiel+36%3A8-12&version=KJV
[8] https://www.biblegateway.com/passage/?search=ezekiel+37%3A11-14&version=KJV
[9] https://www.biblegateway.com/passage/?search=Ezekiel+38&version=KJV
[10] https://promisedlandministries.wordpress.com/2010/03/14/shadows-of-the-messiah-where-gods-name-is-written/
[11] http://www.whatsgoingonnews.net/study-tools
[12] https://www.biblegateway.com/passage/?search=ezekiel+39&version=KJV
[13] http://www.joelstrumpet.com/?p=2681
[14] https://www.biblegateway.com/passage/?search=genesis+10%3A2-3&version=KJV
[15] https://www.biblegateway.com/passage/?search=genesis+10%3A6-7&version=KJV
[16] https://www.biblegateway.com/passage/?search=Ezekiel+39%3A7&version=KJV
[17] https://www.biblegateway.com/passage/?search=Ezekiel+39%3A13&version=KJV
[18] https://www.biblegateway.com/passage/?search=Ezekiel+39%3A21&version=KJV
[19] https://www.blueletterbible.org/kjv/eze/38/18/t_conc_840018
[20] https://www.blueletterbible.org/kjv/eze/38/18/t_conc_840019
[21] http://www.studylight.org/desk/interlinear.cgi?search_form_type=interlinear&q1=Ezekiel+38%3A18&ot=lxx&nt=wh&s=0&t3=str_nas&ns=0

[22] http://www.studylight.org/desk/interlinear.cgi?search_form_type=interlinear&q1=Ezekiel+38%3A19&ot=lxx&nt=wh&s=0&t3=str_nas&ns=0
[23] https://www.blueletterbible.org/kjv/rev/16/19/t_conc_1183019
[24] https://www.biblegateway.com/passage/?search=I+Thessalonians+5%3A5%2C+9-10&version=KJV
[25] https://www.biblegateway.com/passage/?search=Ezekiel+39&version=KJV
[26] http://biblehub.com/commentaries/ezekiel/39-2.htm
[27] http://biblehub.com/hebrew/983.htm
[28] https://www.biblegateway.com/passage/?search=matthew+24&version=KJV
[29] https://www.biblegateway.com/passage/?search=revelation+12&version=KJV
[30] https://www.biblegateway.com/passage/?search=zechariah+13&version=KJV
[31] https://www.biblegateway.com/passage/?search=II+Peter+3&version=KJV
[32] https://www.biblegateway.com/passage/?search=matthew+24&version=KJV
[33] http://biblehub.com/commentaries/ezekiel/39-16.htm
[34] http://biblehub.com/commentaries/ezekiel/39-11.htm
[35] http://www.bible-history.com/maps/5-israel-ancient-inhabitants.html
[36] http://ccat.sas.upenn.edu/nets/edition/38-iezekiel-nets.pdf
[37] http://www.telegraph.co.uk/comment/11844915/A-wall-of-iron-built-to-keep-out-Gog-and-Magog.html
[38] http://biblehub.com/commentaries/ezekiel/38-2.htm
[39] https://www.biblegateway.com/passage/?search=II+Corinthians+5&version=KJV
[40] https://www.biblegateway.com/passage/?search=revelation+11&version=KJV
[41] https://www.biblegateway.com/passage/?search=romans+11&version=KJV
[42] https://www.biblegateway.com/passage/?search=galatians+3&version=KJV
[43] https://www.biblegateway.com/passage/?search=romans+11&version=KJV
[44] https://www.biblegateway.com/passage/?search=II+Thessalonians+2&version=KJV
[45] https://gracethrufaith.com/end-times-prophecy/ezekiel-38-39-overview-and-summary/
[46] https://www.biblegateway.com/passage/?search=daniel+9&version=KJV
[47] http://www.khouse.org/enews_article/2007/1190/print/
[48] https://www.biblegateway.com/passage/?search=matthew+21&version=KJV
[49] http://www.chabad.org/library/article_cdo/aid/108400/jewish/The-End-of-Days.htm
[50] http://www.studylight.org/desk/interlinear.cgi?search_form_type=interlinear&q1=Daniel+9%3A27&ot=lxx&nt=wh&s=0&t3=str_kjv&ns=0

[51] http://www.studylight.org/desk/interlinear.cgi?search_form_type=interlinear&q1=Daniel+9%3A27&ot=lxx&nt=wh&s=0&t3=str_kjv&ns=0

[52] https://www.blueletterbible.org/lang/lexicon/lexicon.cfm?Strongs=G1412&t=KJV

[53] https://www.biblegateway.com/passage/?search=colossians+1&version=KJV

[54] https://www.blueletterbible.org/kjv/col/1/11/t_conc_1108011

[55] https://www.blueletterbible.org/lang/lexicon/lexicon.cfm?page=2&strongs=G1411&t=KJV#lexResults

[56] https://www.biblegateway.com/passage/?search=revelation+13&version=KJV

[57] https://www.biblegateway.com/passage/?search=john+5&version=KJV

[58] https://www.biblegateway.com/passage/?search=I+Thessalonians+5&version=KJV

[59] http://www.bridalcovenant.com/wedding1.html

[60] https://www.biblegateway.com/passage/?search=Revelation%2012&version=KJV

[61] https://www.blueletterbible.org/lang/lexicon/lexicon.cfm?Strongs=H1285&t=KJV

[62] https://gracethrufaith.com/end-times-prophecy/ezekiel-38-39-overview-and-summary/

[63] https://www.biblegateway.com/passage/?search=hebrews+10&version=KJV

[64] https://www.biblegateway.com/passage/?search=Hebrews%209&version=KJV

[65] https://www.biblegateway.com/passage/?search=Isaiah+28&version=KJV

[66] https://www.biblegateway.com/passage/?search=Romans+8:2&version=KJV

[67] https://www.biblegateway.com/passage/?search=1 Corinthians+15:56&version=KJV

[68] https://www.biblegateway.com/passage/?search=Galatians+3&version=KJV

[69] https://www.biblegateway.com/passage/?search=revelation+4&version=KJV

[70] https://www.biblegateway.com/passage/?search=revelation+19&version=KJV

[71] https://www.biblegateway.com/passage/?search=genesis+9%3A13&version=KJV

[72] http://www.studylight.org/desk/interlinear.cgi?search_form_type=interlinear&q1=genesis+9%3A13&ot=lxx&nt=wh&s=0&t3=str_hcs&ns=0

[73] http://www.studylight.org/desk/interlinear.cgi?search_form_type=interlinear&q1=genesis+9%3A13&ot=lxx&nt=wh&s=0&t3=str_hcs&ns=0

[74] https://www.biblegateway.com/passage/?search=II+Thessalonians+2&version=KJV

[75] http://biblehub.com/lexicon/daniel/9-27.htm
[76] http://www.jewishencyclopedia.com/articles/12494-rabbi
[77] https://www.biblegateway.com/passage/?search=isaiah+28&version=KJV
[78] http://biblehub.com/commentaries/isaiah/28-15.htm
[79] https://www.biblegateway.com/passage/?search=revelation+11&version=KJV
[80] https://www.biblegateway.com/passage/?search=hebrews+9&version=KJV
[81] https://www.biblegateway.com/passage/?search=Revelation%2012&version=KJV
[82] https://www.biblegateway.com/passage/?search=exodus+19&version=KJV
[83] https://www.biblegateway.com/passage/?search=matthew+24&version=KJV
[84] https://www.biblegateway.com/passage/?search=Matthew%2023&version=KJV
[85] https://www.biblegateway.com/passage/?search=Revelation+13&version=KJV
[86] https://www.biblegateway.com/passage/?search=daniel+11&version=KJV
[87] https://www.biblegateway.com/passage/?search=II+Thessalonians+2&version=KJV
[88] https://www.biblegateway.com/passage/?search=daniel+7&version=KJV
[89] https://www.biblegateway.com/passage/?search=revelation+19&version=KJV
[90] https://www.biblegateway.com/passage/?search=Matthew%2026&version=KJV
[91] https://www.biblegateway.com/passage/?search=I+Corinthians+15&version=KJV
[92] https://www.biblegateway.com/passage/?search=acts+4&version=KJV
[93] https://www.biblegateway.com/passage/?search=John+14&version=KJV
[94] https://www.biblegateway.com/passage/?search=Leviticus+23&version=KJV
[95] http://biblehub.com/hebrew/4150.htm
[96] http://biblehub.com/hebrew/6944.htm
[97] http://biblehub.com/hebrew/4744.htm
[98] https://www.biblegateway.com/passage/?search=colossians+2&version=KJV
[99] https://www.biblegateway.com/passage/?search=matthew+5&version=KJV
[100] https://www.biblegateway.com/passage/?search=daniel+9&version=KJV
[101] http://www.khouse.org/enews_article/2007/1190/print/
[102] https://www.biblegateway.com/passage/?search=matthew+21&version=KJV
[103] https://www.biblegateway.com/passage/?search=I+Corinthians+5&version=KJV
[104] https://www.biblegateway.com/passage/?search=john+1&version=KJV
[105] https://www.biblegateway.com/passage/?search=Isaiah+53&version=KJV
[106] https://www.biblegateway.com/passage/?search=matthew+27&version=KJV
[107] https://www.biblegateway.com/passage/?search=colossians+2&version=KJV
[108] https://www.biblegateway.com/passage/?search=ephesians+4&version=KJV
[109] https://www.biblegateway.com/passage/?search=matthew+28&version=KJV
[110] https://www.biblegateway.com/passage/?search=I+Corinthians+15&version=KJV

[111] https://www.biblegateway.com/passage/?search=I+Corinthians+15&version=KJV
[112] https://www.biblegateway.com/passage/?search=revelation+3&version=KJV
[113] https://www.blueletterbible.org/lang/lexicon/lexicon.cfm?Strongs=G4005&t=KJV
[114] https://www.biblegateway.com/passage/?search=john+14&version=KJV
[115] https://www.biblegateway.com/passage/?search=acts+1&version=KJV
[116] https://www.biblegateway.com/passage/?search=acts+2&version=KJV
[117] https://www.biblegateway.com/passage/?search=john+14&version=KJV
[118] https://www.biblegateway.com/passage/?search=ephesians+1&version=KJV
[119] https://www.biblegateway.com/passage/?search=romans+8&version=KJV
[120] https://www.biblegateway.com/passage/?search=titus+2&version=KJV
[121] https://www.biblegateway.com/passage/?search=revelation+3&version=KJV
[122] http://biblehub.com/hebrew/2146.htm
[123] https://jewsforjesus.org/publications/newsletter/september-2000/feastoftrumpets
[124] https://www.biblegateway.com/passage/?search=exodus+19&version=KJV
[125] https://jewsforjesus.org/publications/newsletter/september-2000/feastoftrumpets
[126] https://www.biblegateway.com/quicksearch/?quicksearch=trumpet&qs_version=KJV
[127] https://www.biblegateway.com/passage/?search=genesis+49&version=KJV
[128] http://www.1888mpm.org/book/chapter-8-christ-lawgiver
[129] https://www.biblegateway.com/passage/?search=I+thessalonians+4&version=KJV
[130] https://www.biblegateway.com/passage/?search=revelation+4&version=KJV
[131] http://www.oneplace.com/ministries/thru-the-bible-with-j-vernon-mcgee/read/articles/q--a-why-was-jesus-baptized-when-he-had-no-sin-14381.html
[132] https://www.biblegateway.com/passage/?search=Leviticus+16&version=KJV
[133] https://www.biblegateway.com/passage/?search=matthew+3&version=KJV
[134] https://www.biblegateway.com/passage/?search=john+1&version=KJV
[135] https://www.biblegateway.com/passage/?search=matthew+4&version=KJV
[136] https://www.biblegateway.com/passage/?search=I+Timothy+2&version=KJV
[137] https://www.biblegateway.com/passage/?search=hebrews+2&version=KJV
[138] https://www.biblegateway.com/passage/?search=Hebrews+9&version=KJV
[139] http://www.jewfaq.org/holiday5.htm
[140] http://biblehub.com/greek/4637.htm
[141] https://www.biblegateway.com/passage/?search=john+1&version=KJV
[142] https://www.biblegateway.com/passage/?search=luke+2&version=KJV
[143] https://www.biblegateway.com/passage/?search=revelation+19&version=KJV
[144] https://www.biblegateway.com/passage/?search=Daniel+9&version=KJV

[145] https://jewsforjesus.org/issues-v05-n01/the-messianic-time-table-according-to-daniel-the-prophet
[146] https://www.biblegateway.com/passage/?search=II+Timothy+4&version=KJV
[147] https://www.biblegateway.com/passage/?search=matthew+25&version=KJV
[148] https://www.biblegateway.com/passage/?search=joel+3&version=KJV
[149] https://www.biblegateway.com/passage/?search=genesis+12&version=KJV
[150] https://www.biblegateway.com/passage/?search=revelation+19&version=KJV
[151] https://www.biblegateway.com/passage/?search=revelation+16&version=KJV
[152] https://www.biblegateway.com/passage/?search=zechariah+12&version=KJV
[153] https://www.biblegateway.com/passage/?search=micah+2&version=KJV
[154] https://www.biblegateway.com/passage/?search=isaiah+63&version=KJV
[155] https://www.biblegateway.com/passage/?search=revelation+14&version=KJV
[156] https://www.biblegateway.com/passage/?search=john+8&version=KJV
[157] https://www.biblegateway.com/passage/?search=john+1%3A12&version=KJV
[158] https://www.biblegateway.com/passage/?search=I+Thessalonians+5%3A5&version=KJV
[159] https://www.biblegateway.com/passage/?search=matthew+5&version=KJV
[160] https://www.biblegateway.com/passage/?search=I+peter+2%3A9&version=KJV
[151] https://www.biblegateway.com/passage/?search=genesis+1&version=KJV
[162] https://www.biblegateway.com/passage/?search=romans+1%3A20&version=KJV
[163] https://www.biblegateway.com/passage/?search=john+4%3A24&version=KJV
[164] https://www.biblegateway.com/passage/?search=john+1&version=KJV
[165] https://www.biblegateway.com/passage/?search=II+Peter+3%3A10&version=KJV
[165] https://www.biblegateway.com/passage/?search=matthew+24&version=KJV
[167] https://www.biblegateway.com/passage/?search=daniel+7&version=KJV
[168] https://www.biblegateway.com/passage/?search=psalm+82&version=KJV
[169] https://www.biblegateway.com/passage/?search=Isaiah+11:4&version=KJV
[170] https://www.biblegateway.com/passage/?search=revelation+19&version=KJV
[171] https://www.biblegateway.com/passage/?search=II+Thessalonians+2&version=KJV
[172] https://www.biblegateway.com/passage/?search=deuteronomy+4&version=KJV
[173] https://www.biblegateway.com/passage/?search=Zechariah+14&version=KJV
[174] https://www.biblegateway.com/passage/?search=zephaniah+1&version=KJV
[175] https://www.biblegateway.com/passage/?search=joel+2&version=KJV
[176] https://www.biblegateway.com/passage/?search=amos+5&version=KJV
[177] https://www.biblegateway.com/passage/?search=isaiah+60&version=KJV

[178] https://www.biblegateway.com/passage/?search=revelation+16&version=KJV
[179] https://www.biblegateway.com/passage/?search=daniel+9%3A27&version=KJV
[180] https://www.biblegateway.com/passage/?search=daniel+11&version=KJV
[181] https://www.biblegateway.com/passage/?search=daniel+7&version=KJV
[182] https://www.biblegateway.com/passage/?search=matthew+23&version=KJV
[183] https://www.biblegateway.com/passage/?search=hosea+5&version=KJV
[184] https://www.biblegateway.com/passage/?search=zechariah+13&version=KJV
[185] https://www.biblegateway.com/passage/?search=isaiah+59&version=KJV
[186] https://www.biblegateway.com/passage/?search=joel+2&version=KJV
[187] https://www.biblegateway.com/passage/?search=romans+11&version=KJV
[188] https://www.biblegateway.com/passage/?search=Jeremiah+31%3A31-34&version=KJV
[189] https://www.biblegateway.com/passage/?search=romans+9&version=KJV
[190] https://www.biblegateway.com/passage/?search=galatians+3&version=KJV
[191] https://www.biblegateway.com/passage/?search=hebrews+11&version=KJV
[192] http://biblehub.com/text/daniel/9-24.htm
[193] https://www.biblegateway.com/passage/?search=zechariah+6&version=KJV
[194] https://www.biblegateway.com/passage/?search=hebrews+7&version=KJV
[195] https://www.biblegateway.com/passage/?search=hebrews4&version=KJV
[196] https://www.biblegateway.com/passage/?search=Hebrews+9&version=KJV
[197] https://www.biblegateway.com/passage/?search=Hebrews+10&version=KJV
[198] https://www.biblegateway.com/passage/?search=colossians+2&version=KJV
[199] https://www.biblegateway.com/passage/?search=I+Corinthians+15&version=KJV
[200] https://www.biblegateway.com/passage/?search=hebrews+10&version=KJV
[201] https://www.biblegateway.com/passage/?search=daniel+2&version=KJV
[202] https://www.biblegateway.com/passage/?search=psalm+118&version=KJV
[203] https://www.biblegateway.com/passage/?search=I+Peter+2&version=KJV
[204] https://www.biblegateway.com/passage/?search=Ephesians+2:20&version=KJV
[205] https://www.biblegateway.com/passage/?search=Daniel+4&version=KJV
[206] https://www.biblegateway.com/passage/?search=Daniel+7&version=KJV
[207] https://www.biblegateway.com/passage/?search=psalm+2&version=KJV
[208] https://www.biblegateway.com/passage/?search=hebrews+10&version=KJV
[209] https://www.biblegateway.com/passage/?search=matthew+4&version=KJV
[210] https://www.biblegateway.com/passage/?search=micah+5&version=KJV
[211] https://www.biblegateway.com/passage/?search=isaiah+9&version=KJV
[212] https://www.biblegateway.com/passage/?search=isaiah+16&version=KJV
[213] https://www.biblegateway.com/passage/?search=luke+1&version=KJV
[214] https://www.biblegateway.com/passage/?search=Revelation+20&version=KJV
[215] https://www.biblegateway.com/passage/?search=isaiah+1&version=KJV

[216] https://www.biblegateway.com/passage/?search=isaiah+32&version=KJV
[217] https://www.biblegateway.com/passage/?search=jeremiah+23&version=KJV
[218] https://www.biblegateway.com/passage/?search=Isaiah+61&version=KJV
[219] https://www.biblegateway.com/passage/?search=II+Peter+3&version=KJV
[220] https://www.biblegateway.com/passage/?search=revelation+19&version=KJV
[221] https://www.biblegateway.com/passage/?search=2%20Chronicles+5&version=KJV
[222] https://www.biblegateway.com/passage/?search=2+Chronicles+7&version=KJV
[223] https://www.biblegateway.com/passage/?search=haggai+2&version=KJV
[224] https://www.biblegateway.com/passage/?search=luke+2&version=KJV
[225] https://www.biblegateway.com/passage/?search=zechariah+6&version=KJV
[226] https://www.biblegateway.com/passage/?search=isaiah+53&version=KJV
[227] https://www.biblegateway.com/passage/?search=Matthew+16&version=KJV
[228] https://www.biblegateway.com/passage/?search=I+Corinthians+3&version=KJV
[229] https://www.biblegateway.com/quicksearch/?quicksearch=lively+stone&qs_version=KJV
[230] https://www.biblegateway.com/passage/?search=ezekiel+43&version=KJV
[231] http://www.studylight.org/desk/interlinear.cgi?search_form_type=interlinear&q1=Leviticus+25%3A10&ot=lxx&nt=wh&s=0&t3=str_nas&ns=0
[232] https://www.blueletterbible.org/lang/lexicon/lexicon.cfm?Strongs=G859&t=KJV
[233] https://www.biblegateway.com/passage/?search=Colossians+1&version=KJV
[234] https://www.biblegateway.com/passage/?search=Ephesians+1&version=KJV
[235] https://www.biblegateway.com/passage/?search=luke+4&version=KJV
[236] https://www.biblegateway.com/passage/?search=revelation+5&version=KJV
[237] http://biblehub.com/greek/59.htm
[238] https://www.biblegateway.com/passage/?search=II+Corinthians+5%3A17&version=KJV
[239] https://www.biblegateway.com/passage/?search=Ephesians+4&version=KJV
[240] https://www.biblegateway.com/passage/?search=Ephesians+1&version=KJV
[241] https://www.biblegateway.com/passage/?search=romans+8&version=KJV
[242] https://www.biblegateway.com/passage/?search=romans+11&version=KJV
[243] http://www.khouse.org/articles/2006/683/
[244] https://www.biblegateway.com/passage/?search=ezekiel+40%3A1&version=KJV
[245] https://www.biblegateway.com/passage/?search=jeremiah+46&version=KJV

[246] https://www.biblegateway.com/passage/?search=daniel+1&version=KJV
[247] http://www.berenddeboer.net/sab/dan/1.html
[248] https://en.wikipedia.org/wiki/James_Ussher
[249] http://www.berenddeboer.net/sab/dan/1.html
[250] https://answersingenesis.org/ministry-news/ministry/appendix-b-the-forgotten-archbishop/
[251] https://www.biblegateway.com/passage/?search=Exodus+16&version=KJV
[252] https://www.biblegateway.com/passage/?search=exodus+16&version=KJV
[253] https://www.biblegateway.com/passage/?search=deuteronomy+1&version=KJV
[254] https://www.biblegateway.com/passage/?search=joshua+5&version=KJV
[255] http://biblehub.com/commentaries/exodus/16-35.htm
[256] https://www.biblegateway.com/passage/?search=I+kings+6%3A1&version=KJV
[257] https://www.biblegateway.com/passage/?search=II+chronicles+9&version=KJV
[258] http://www.bibleprophecyblog.com/2009/04/passover-coronation-day-for-jewish.html
[259] https://www.biblegateway.com/passage/?search=I+kings+6%3A1&version=KJV
[260] https://www.biblegateway.com/passage/?search=matthew+28&version=KJV

Printed in Great Britain
by Amazon